Men
My Mother
Dated

and Other
Mostly True Tales

Villard  New York

Brett Leveridge

Men
My Mother
Dated

and Other
Mostly True Tales

All rights reserved under International and Pan-American Copyright Conventions.
Published in the United States by Villard Books, a division of Random House, Inc.,
New York, and simultaneously in Canada by Random House of Canada Limited, Toronto.

VILLARD BOOKS and colophon are registered trademarks of Random House, Inc.

Most of the essays that appear in this work were originally published in Might *magazine*
and/or on the author's website, BRETTnews (www.brettnews.com). In addition,
"How I Learned to Stop Worrying and Love Massage" originally appeared on the
Urban Desires website (www.desires.com); "My Dinner with Charla" and "Gay Like Me"
originally appeared www.tripod.com; and "Crying Uncle on Fatherhood" first appeared
in The Oklahoma Gazette. *"When Animals Attack Bob Saget," "The Curse of Cupid,"*
and "See You in September" were all broadcast on the program All Things Considered
on National Public Radio.

The photographs on pages 72 (bottom), 80 (top), 127, and 168 are from the author's
collection. The photo on page 9 is courtesy Archive Photos; the photos on pages 74 and
147 are courtesy Frank Driggs/Archive Photos. All other photos are courtesy Superstock.

Library of Congress Cataloging-in-Publication data is available.

ISBN 0-375-50400-1

Random House website address: www.villard.com

Printed in the United States of America on acid-free paper

2 4 6 8 9 7 5 3

First Edition

Book design by Karolina Harris

To Lloyd and Karen

Legal Disclaimer

This is a work of fiction. In the legal sense. I mean, you know how lawyers are: Either it's 100 percent true or it must be fiction. But what is truth? You've seen Rashomon, *right? No? Oh, you really must see it, it's one of Kurosawa's best. Anyway, in* Rashomon, *there's this rape-murder, and four people who witnessed it each offer an account of the incident, and of course they all differ. So say, for example, that the author's mom, years before the author is even a twinkle in her eye, goes out to dinner with a guy named Pete. They go out for Italian. Their waiter is named Herman. And the coat-check girl's name is Velma. At one point, Mom stands up, spills red wine all over the table, gives Pete a good hard slap across the face, and storms out of the restaurant. Now, if you were to ask Pete what happened, his version would probably differ greatly from Mom's. And Herman, who's waited on Pete before and knows him to be a rather chintzy tipper and who only saw the spillage and slappage from the corner of his eye while he was taking an order at another table anyway, would have still another account. And Velma, who thinks Pete one gorgeous hunk of man and who was watching the pair from the moment they sat down in an attempt to ascertain whether Pete and that cheap blonde were actually on a date or if they were just friends or first cousins or something, would offer another story altogether.*

So the reader is advised to think of the accounts in this book as one woman's recollections of dates that occurred many years ago filtered through the overactive imagination of her no-account son, the author. No doubt the men Mom dated would offer different versions of the events detailed in this collection. As would the various waiters, cabdrivers, landladies, ticket sellers, and other peripheral characters who appear in these tales. And that's just fine; let 'em all write their own damn books. Because, like we said, these stories are, in the legal sense, works of fiction. Like every love story ever told. But the essays and stories that follow them, the ones taken from the author's own life? Those are true. Mostly.

Foreword

I first met Brett Leveridge at Mickey Mantle's restaurant in New York City. I was seated at a booth in the far corner of the restaurant's main room, and he arrived, pen and pad in hand, ready to take my order.

He had an Oklahoma accent (fitting for someone working at Mantle's); more to the point, he saw to it that my burger came out just the way I ordered it: medium rare, topped with American cheese, pickle and tomato on the side. Not that getting this straight was brain surgery, but I appreciated it nonetheless.

As it happened, Brett would wait on me any number of other times in the ensuing months. I'd stop into Mantle's for a bite and often as not find myself seated in his section. The routine was always the same: attentive (but not fawning) service, a little sports talk, and a tasty meal—simple pleasures that I came to take for granted.

A good waiter—one who can be relied upon to get you a burger and a beer with a minimum of fuss—is a craftsman to be cherished. But in a city like New York, it's a rare service worker indeed who doesn't have his or her eye on a larger prize. The cabdriver who brings you in from the airport is probably hard at work on his third symphony; the doorman at your hotel likely spends his nights slaving over a script he's certain will one day win an Oscar; and the waiter who serves you at your favorite little café does so only to pay his bills and bide his time between auditions.

And writers outnumber them all; the city's crawling with would-be playwrights, journalists, novelists, and other assorted scribes. You can't throw a fastball in Manhattan without hitting one. So I wasn't particularly surprised when Brett presented, at the end of a meal, not only my check but a copy of his zine, *BRETTnews*. Here were twelve photocopied pages filled with essays, tall tales, slightly skewed horoscopes, and quirky advice columns that surely no one would heed. It was clever stuff, and I enjoyed reading it.

But little did I realize that that issue of *BRETTnews* was a presage to the end of a perfectly satisfying diner-waiter relationship. By 1994, Brett had taken his publication online, and things really started to take off. His "Men My Mother Dated" was a regular column in *Might* magazine; he was profiled in a cover story for *Virtual City* magazine; he made a pair of appearances on the popular radio program *This American Life* and delivered several humorous commentaries on National Public Radio's *All Things Considered*.

It wasn't long before Brett had moved on from Mickey Mantle's and begun working as a freelance writer and as an editor for various online operations. Still, I held out hope that the whole online thing would be just a fad, that the Web might peter out, that perhaps Brett would return to Mickey Mantle's, where I might again enjoy a burger, a beer, and a bit—but just a bit—of sports talk under his attentive watch. That's not so much to ask, is it?

Alas, the publication of this book probably signals the final dashing of those modest hopes—the end of an era. So, go ahead—enjoy the book you now hold in your hands. Thrill to Brett's mom's romantic adventures. Chuckle at his accounts of life in New York City. Nod in assent as he offers contrarian views on most of the major holidays. While you're at it, why not buy a few copies of this reasonably priced volume for your friends and family? Your mom would probably love a copy, no? Your aunt Edna? Your mailman? They could all use a good laugh, I'm sure. And Brett could certainly use the sales, right? By all means! Let's put Mr. Too-Good-to-Serve-a-Burger on the damned bestseller lists!

And as you page through this book, don't give a thought to my pain and disappointment. After all, I'll no doubt be seated again, one day soon, in that booth in the far corner of the main room at Mantle's. But it won't be the same, because Brett won't be serving me. And you, in a small but undeniable way, will be to blame.

I hope you can live with that.

Bob Costas
March 2000

Acknowledgments

OVER the past nine years, it's become apparent to me that someone else is driving this bus, that I am only a passenger along for the ride. I would be remiss if I did not thank the many people who have appeared, often unexpectedly, to point me in the right direction, to share their wisdom, to offer encouragement.

The wondrous Jyl Elizabeth Brewer performed the miracle of opening my eyes to life's unimagined possibilities, a kindness for which I shall always be in her debt.

It was Michael Lane, an all-but-total stranger, who encouraged me to begin writing and, more specifically, to launch the print edition of my humble little rag, *BRETTnews.* He gave me, a floundering lapsed actor, a fresh start—no small thing, that.

Seth Barrish, a true gentleman, patiently provided my entrée into the world of computers, a life-altering largess if there ever was one.

The very wise Kyle Shannon convinced me in the very early days of the medium that *BRETTnews* belonged on the Web. It was wise counsel, and I thank him for it.

The preternaturally talented Dave Eggers was kind enough to bring my column, "Men My Mother Dated," to a wider audience in his gone-but-not-forgotten publication, *Might* magazine. Long may he wave.

Ira Glass and the other fine people at *This American Life* were kind enough to ask me to appear, and more than once, on their wonderful program. They even offered me the rare opportunity to be rendered in pen-and-ink (thanks, Jessica Abel!) in the *This American Life* comic book—a true embarrassment of riches!

Jeff Rogers and my other friends at *All Things Considered* have been exceedingly good to me. They commissioned a commentary on "shockumentary" television and have since allowed me to appear on their terrific show on several occasions. I am very pleased and proud to be associated with them.

Stacy Horn, Hadley Taylor, Josh Chu, and the other hardworking magicians at echonyc.com have hosted and supported brettnews.com for more than five years running. My deepest thanks to them all.

Jonathan Trumper and Lisa Shotland were kind enough to bring me into the fold of the William Morris Agency and to introduce me to my dedicated and loyal literary agent and friend, Claudia Cross. I thank them all for the enduring faith they've shown in me.

Caitlin Dixon was a calming influence during the anxious weeks that this book was being pitched, and a helpful editorial voice as I completed the writing of it, and for both, I thank her very much.

Marianne Petit, a gifted artist possessed of a saint's patience, has been there for me more times than I can count. She's aces in my book.

Jessie Weiner, video editor extraordinaire and friend to the clueless, generously lent her gift for splendiferous splicing. I thank my lucky stars that I know her.

Bob Costas has been supportive and encouraging of my work since the earliest days of *BRETTnews*. I doubt I can ever properly repay him, but he has my undying gratitude.

Annie Leibovitz shared with me her unique artistry. Never have I been more moved by a gift.

Rarely has a first-time author been so fortunate in being paired with an editor. The utterly singular Lee Boudreaux has treated me so wonderfully; I shall always be thankful to her and her colleagues at Villard for the yeoman's job they have done in supporting my humble efforts.

So many family members and friends, too numerous to name here, have been there for me over the years, urging me on, believing in me. They know who they are, and they have my deepest thanks.

My dear parents—my best friends, my greatest blessings—have stood by me through thick and thin. They've taught me the value of faith, loyalty, and courage. Whoever I am, whatever I accomplish, I owe to them. Theirs is an admirable and lasting legacy of love.

I would also like to thank my beloved grandfather Cecil Oakes. I wish you were here to see this, Granddad.

Contents

Men My Mother Dated

Other Mostly True Tales

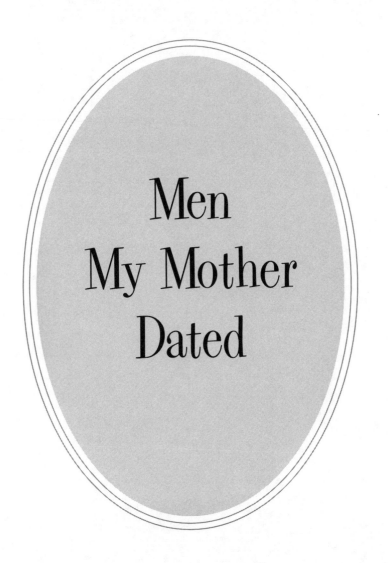

Men
My Mother
Dated

Bob Petronick

MOM'S one date with Bob Petronick, in her freshman year of college, was an eventful evening of firsts. He escorted her to her first fraternity party, a semiformal affair at which she imbibed the first beer of her young life. One beer led to another and then a third, and in short order, she was pretty tight. Another female party goer bumped into her there in the crowded ballroom, and before anything could be done, she and Mom became embroiled in a hair-pulling, eye-gouging catfight, the first such row Mom had ever been involved in.

The fight was broken up by the campus police. Mom's arrest (her first) on drunk-and-disorderly charges led to her first night in jail. Bob, much to his credit, took up a collection around the fraternity house and posted her bail the next morning, but he never called for another date. Mom garnered thirty hours' community service, six months' probation, and a reputation.

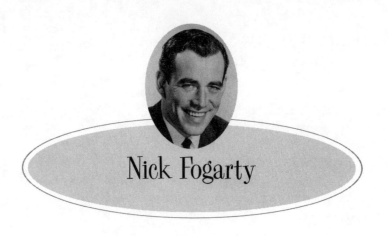

Nick Fogarty

MY parents married some four months after they became formally engaged. Mom, as most of us would, experienced the occasional bout of cold feet during this time of waiting. It was during one of these periods of uncertainty that the company for which she worked as a secretary, Garrett Grommet Corp., hired a new director of sales.

His name was Nick Fogarty, and, oh, was he smooth. He began to ply Mom with sweet talk from the day he set foot in the corporate headquarters, and he never let up. Normally, Mom would easily have dismissed the lines of such a slickster, but in her erratic emotional state, she was vulnerable to his attentions.

After two weeks of pressure, she finally gave in and met Nick for a Tom Collins at Zasu's Paradise Lounge, not far from the office. He was quite charming, and perhaps sensing Mom's trepidation, he behaved in gentlemanly fashion. Mom drove home in a fog, more confused than ever. Sure, she loved her fiancé, the man who was to be my father, but was he the man she should marry? Perhaps she was too young to settle down. And what of Nick? He was so worldly, so exciting.

Her answers came the next day at the office, when she picked up the phone to have a sandwich delivered for lunch and inadvertently selected Line 2 instead of Line 1. Nick was on Line 2, reassuring his wife—his *wife*?!—that he'd not forgotten their fifth anniversary and professing his undying love and devotion.

Trembling at the thought that she might have thrown over my father for such a louse, Mom marched into Nick's office, told him the jig was up, and informed him, in no uncertain terms, that he was to refrain from speaking to her in the future, or she would go straight to Mr. Garrett with all the sordid details of Nick's behavior.

It wasn't until two years later that Mom revealed to Dad her brush with disaster. Dad was, of course, furious with Nick, with whom he'd chatted baseball as recently as the previous summer's office picnic. Not being the violent sort, however, he fought off the urge to give Nick a sound thrashing, opting instead to drop by his house every night for two weeks, ring his doorbell, and run.

Vic Rombozzi

MOM was generally attracted to wholesome, boy-next-door types, but even she was occasionally drawn to the dark side.

Perhaps the shadiest of the men she dated was one Vic Rombozzi. She met Vic during a brief rebellious period in her freshman year of college. A bit older than Mom, he was a member of the school's maintenance staff, assigned to Williams Hall, a building comprising a number of large lecture halls, one of which hosted Mom's U.S. history class.

She'd never really noticed Vic before, but as she stepped out of the lecture hall one brisk October afternoon, he stepped up to light her cigarette (Mom had only just begun smoking, and she usually fumbled a bit with her brand-new Zippo, leaving plenty of time for an opportunistic young man to slip in with a proffered flame).

She thanked Vic for the light and, since it appeared he was not going to wander away, nervously began to make small talk. Vic was not much of a talker, and it fell to Mom to fill the silence between them as she took note of Vic's unusual appearance. He was only five foot three, several inches shorter than Mom, and his hair was long, excessively oiled, and swept back on the sides. He called the look a D.A., and it was only some years later that Mom learned that D.A. stood for "duck's ass." And even today he holds the record among all Mom's suitors for sideburn length.

Vic smoked Lucky Strikes, and as he reached with his left arm for the pack that he kept rolled up in his right shirtsleeve, Mom caught a glimpse of a tattoo. She couldn't quite make out the image etched there on his arm, but it didn't really matter. She'd never known anyone with a tattoo before, and she resolved then and there to get to know Vic.

And in the brief time she knew him, she did manage to break down just a bit the wall he'd erected around himself. She learned that he was from New York City and had come to Oklahoma because he had an aunt there who would put him up while, as he put it, he let the heat die down back there. Mom never did figure out exactly what he meant by that, but it sounded foreboding and dark and even dangerous, and on those occasions when Vic would take Mom in his arms and kiss her, she grew weak in the knees. By mid-November, she was already planning to take Vic home to Okemah for Thanksgiving break. She wasn't at all sure her parents would approve of him, but she wanted to show him off to her friends back home. There was no one like Vic in Okemah, and she knew that he would create a buzz in her tiny hometown.

But he didn't meet her after her history class the next Monday, and he wasn't there on Wednesday either. He had always refused to give her his phone number, something she wrote off as just a quirk, so worried that he might be ill, she stopped by the campus's maintenance offices to inquire after him.

Vic no longer worked for the university, she was told. It seems that he'd been running an on-campus bookie operation, taking bets on college football games from students. When he approached the university's star running back, Dean Seeman, about throwing that weekend's big game against their cross-state rivals, the Oklahoma Sooners, the player blew the whistle on Vic, and he'd taken it on the lam.

Did he return to New York City? Mom has never known. She did receive a letter from Vic during her senior year, though. He was doing five-to-ten in an Iowa prison for passing bad checks, and he wrote to ask Mom for $140 to retain his lawyer's services for another appeal. Mom, no longer the naïve freshman, tossed the letter into the trash, and she never heard from Vic again.

Jack Kerouac

THE summer before her junior year of college, Mom began to crave new surroundings. Although she needed to spend that summer, as she had the previous two, earning money for college, she felt that if she didn't get away from Okemah, she'd go insane.

My grandfather, recalling the impatient restlessness he'd experienced in his own youth, was sympathetic to Mom's plight and convinced my grandmother, who was at first skeptical, to call her sister Ruth on Mom's behalf.

Aunt Ruth was the nearest approximation to a bohemian to be found in the Larsen branch of the family. At that, she did not live so very far outside society's norm; she was married, after all, and lived not in San Francisco, New York, or Paris but in hot, dusty Amarillo, Texas. But Ruth was an artist, a painter whose work vacillated between O'Keeffian landscapes depicting the bluffs and cliffs of West Texas and eastern New Mexico and simple constructions of triangles and squares in various shades of red, purple, and blue.

Ruth and her husband, Ben, had recently opened a combination filling station/café just east of town, at the intersection of
U.S. Route 66 and State Highway 370. They hired a local Mexican
couple to operate the café (which doubled as a gallery to display
Ruth's paintings), serving enchiladas, tamales, and burgers, while
Ben pumped gas and did minor repair work and tune-ups for
travelers bound for the West Coast, preparing their vehicles for
the strenuous journey through the deserts of New Mexico, Arizona, and California. Ruth agreed to have Mom spend the summer with them, living in the guest room of their modest home a
mile from the station and waiting tables in the café/gallery.

Mom was a good waitress, at once efficient and friendly, and
usually managed to sock away between ten and fifteen dollars in
tips per shift. It was her plan to move out of the dorms that fall
and into an apartment, and to do so she knew she'd have to
amass a sizable sum over the summer. So she worked as many
hours as Ruth and Ben would allow.

During the summer vacation season, the café was open
twenty-four hours a day. Many travelers preferred to tackle the
long drive through New Mexico and Arizona in the cooler hours
of night and early morning. One Saturday found Mom working
the counter for the 4:00 A.M.-to-noon shift. She'd just slipped on
her apron when in walked a bedraggled trio of young men.

The threesome sidled up to the counter and slid onto the
stools. One, a blue-eyed, brown-haired, square-jawed man of
perhaps twenty-one, dressed in blue jeans and a T-shirt yel-
lowed by perspiration, looked exhausted; he barely glanced at
the menu before plopping his head facedown onto his arms,
which were resting, crisscrossed, on the Formica counter.

His companions, though bleary-eyed, had a bit more energy and showed a decided interest in the menu's offerings. One was a dark-haired, very attractive man who was by far the more gregarious of the two; he seemed relatively unaffected by their stint on the road and the early hour. Mom had gained a certain facility for placing accents while working at the café, and this fellow's rapid-fire way of speaking suggested to her that he hailed from somewhere back East—New York, perhaps, or Boston. His name, as he soon informed Mom, was Jack. He introduced the man dozing facedown as his pal Neal; the third member of the party, a slim, soft-spoken young man whose right arm was swollen to a rather alarming extent from, as he explained it, a wasp sting suffered just south of Denver, was named Frank.

Jack roused Neal just long enough to extract his order: scrambled eggs, bacon, hash browns, and coffee. Frank opted for fried eggs and sausage patties. Jack asked for enchiladas and was visibly disappointed when Mom informed him that they were not available at that hour. Unlike most of the weary travelers who stumbled into the café, these three were headed south on 370, not west on 66; they were bound for Mexico City, Jack explained, and he'd had his heart set on enchiladas for the last hundred miles or more. He finally persuaded Pedro, the short-order cook on duty that early morning, to grill him a cheeseburger with jalapeño peppers.

Soon the food was served, and all three ate voraciously. Neal, immediately upon polishing off his eggs and bacon, returned to the Ford and slept in the backseat. Frank, who was feverish from the insect bite, joined him soon thereafter, sliding into the front seat.

Jack, it seemed, required no sleep. He was far too excited about the prospects of their journey south of the border. They were to visit their friend Bill, he explained, who was living in Mexico City with his wife, Joan. Jack, who professed himself a writer, was eager to experience a new culture, see a new way of life, hear new sounds, smell new smells.

Suddenly realizing he'd talked of little but himself, Jack turned the conversation to Mom's life, peppering her with questions. What was her hometown like? What were her dreams? Where had she been? What had she experienced? What had brought her to Amarillo? Had she ever been in love? What music did she listen to? Though his interest seemed sincere, Mom began to feel embarrassed, fearing that she had no compelling answers to his questions, that her life had been typical and conventional compared with Jack's. Though he was only a couple of years older than she, Jack seemed infinitely more worldly. He'd been in the navy and the merchant marine; he'd lived in New York City, driven cross-country more than once, spent time in New Orleans, San Francisco, Denver, and Los Angeles; he'd even been in jail, charged as an accessory to a murder (a bum rap, he insisted, and one he'd beaten).

Mom found herself utterly smitten by this alien being, this fast-talking, hard-living man of the world. When Jack suggested that they step out behind the café and watch the sunrise, Mom asked Pedro to cover for her while she took a break. The café's only other customer at the time was a truck driver who'd already eaten and was loading up on coffee before hitting the road.

They sat in the tall grass on the gentle downward slope of the hill behind the café, and Jack spoke of his childhood in Lowell,

Massachusetts—how he'd grown up shy and awkward, how he'd found his confidence on the football field, and how he hoped to soon conquer the literary world, to become, as he put it, a "Beat Tolstoy." Mom hadn't a clue what he meant by that, but, while feeling that she was perhaps in a bit over her head, she nodded as if she understood.

Mom was struck by Jack's fluid mix of confidence and insecurity. He revealed that Neal was, to him, a bit of a hero. He envied Neal's spontaneous, gregarious approach to life, his refusal to apologize for who he was and what he did. Neal occasionally hurt those he claimed to care for, Jack admitted—Jack himself, it seemed, had more than once been the victim of Neal's thoughtless self-centeredness. But Neal was on to something, Jack insisted, and Jack was trying to learn everything he could from him.

To Mom, Jack seemed in that moment like a small, unsure boy who worshipped an uncle or older brother. It was a remarkably appealing side to this man she'd only just met, and when he leaned over to gently kiss first her palm and then her cheek and finally her lips, she did not resist.

Before long, though, Jack reached in his pocket for a cigarette lighter and an odd-looking brown cigarette. It was pot, he explained—marijuana. Would she like to try it? Mom knew almost nothing of marijuana—she'd certainly never seen anyone smoke it—and though she felt safe with Jack, she couldn't bring herself to try it.

Jack took a couple of long, deep hits from the cigarette before tamping it out in the dew-moistened ground and placing it back in his pocket. He began to speak again of the coming adventures in Mexico. Had Mom ever been, he wondered? Had she ever wanted to go?

Suddenly Mom had the distinct impression that Jack was about to ask her to accompany him to Mexico City, and she felt a flutter of excited indecision in the pit of her stomach as she wondered how she might respond to such a proposition. It would be the most outrageous leap she'd ever allowed herself, that much was certain, but after all, she was nearly twenty-one; perhaps she was overdue for a bit of adventure.

She had all but convinced herself to accept Jack's offer, should it be tendered, when Pedro appeared at the back door of the café, looking terribly worried. The West Texas wind quickly carried his alarums the fifty or more yards that stood between him and Mom and Jack. "Señorita!" he exclaimed. "Señorita, come quick!" Mom hadn't a clue how long they'd been out there—she'd let time get completely away from her—and her mind raced as she ran back to the café, Jack only a few steps behind her. What could be wrong? Had Pedro started a grease fire in the kitchen, as he had done twice already in the brief time Mom had been in Amarillo? Was the café being robbed?

As she rushed through the kitchen, where nothing was aflame, and out into the dining room, she saw that Neal and Frank had returned from their nap in the Ford. The jukebox was turned up full blast, blaring one of the *conjunto* records that Ben had stocked to keep the kitchen staff happy during the long, slow overnight hours. Neal—stripped to the waist, a lit cigarette in one hand and a half-empty bottle of tequila in the other—was dancing furiously on the tabletop in the rearmost booth. In his dervishian glee, Neal had kicked the ketchup bottle, the sugar dispenser, the salt and pepper shakers, and the tiny container of Tabasco to the floor, creating a treacherous, shard-filled slick. Frank, who Mom had thought so meek and shy, sat two booths away, egging Neal on, shouting, "Go, baby, go!"

Just then, through the café's large front windows, Mom spotted her uncle Ben ambling across the parking lot. He'd arrived early on this Saturday and would be at the front door in just moments. Ben was a soft-spoken man, but he had a quick temper and she hated to think how he might react when he came upon this scene.

She shoved Jack into action, urging him to gather his friends and make a hasty exit.

Now Ben was standing, mouth agape, in the café's entryway. He quickly stepped behind the cashier's stand at the front of the store and retrieved the baseball bat he kept there for emergencies. Workers from nearby oil fields made a practice of breakfasting at the café after a night of carousing, and he'd occasionally had to brandish—though never actually use—the bat to break up a drunken skirmish. Mom doubted he would really use the bat now, but Jack clearly had no intention of waiting around to find out. He pulled Neal down from the tabletop with one hand, hauled the drunken Frank out of his booth with the other, and dragged them both through the front door.

Ben let the trio pass unhindered, but he followed them out the door, bat in hand, to ensure that they were truly on their way. Mom was right behind him. The last glimpse she caught of Jack was his laughing face as he pointed the Ford south on 370 toward Childress. His left arm jutting out the window, he pounded the roof of the car in delight over their narrow escape.

Mom hadn't thought of Jack in years when, nearly a decade later, she spied his picture in a bookstore, on the jacket of a novel entitled *On the Road.* He hadn't been lying, she realized; Jack really was a writer.

In the ensuing weeks she saw interviews and profiles of Jack in magazines and newspapers; she even happened to catch, purely by chance, his appearance on *The Steve Allen Show.* He seemed somehow changed since that morning on the hill behind the café—less insecure somehow, but also less gentle and therefore less charming. Still, Mom, now married with two young sons, knew that she was no longer the girl he'd kissed that morning long ago, so she supposed it wasn't fair to expect Jack to remain unchanged. She bought a copy of *On the Road* and found its breathless style not really to her liking. And when she skipped ahead to Jack's account of the Mexico City journey, she was a bit saddened to learn that somehow he'd neglected to mention her in the book. Had it been a conscious bit of self-editing on Jack's part, or had he simply forgotten their encounter?

Even now, on those occasions when her travels take her through the Texas Panhandle, Mom makes it a point to seek out the junction of old Route 66 and Highway 370, since renamed 287. Though the café is long gone, Mom parks the car and wanders down the slope of the hill where once it stood; she sits in the tall grass and spends a few minutes thinking of poor Jack Kerouac, whose circumstances turned so sad, and wondering how different her own life might have been if Neal's drunken antics hadn't prevented Jack from whisking her off to Mexico City on that cool, sunny morning all those years ago.

Tommy Sewell

MOM spent her twenty-third birthday in the company of girlfriends. Their plan was to treat her to her very first taste of pizza pie at Ned's Pizzeria and then stop in the nearby Linger Lounge for a cocktail or two.

Aside from scorching the roof of her mouth on the hot tomato sauce, Mom's first encounter with pizza was a successful one, the beginning of what would turn out to be a long and satisfying relationship. And she was quite smitten as well with the waiter who served that pie, a gorgeous young man by the name of Tommy Sewell. Tommy had curly black hair, dark brown eyes, and the longest eyelashes Mom had ever seen on a man.

Her pals wasted no time in making Tommy aware that it was Mom's birthday, and he made quite a fuss over her. She couldn't at first decide if his flirty attention was meant to inspire a generous tip or if he was truly attracted to her. As the group gathered their things to leave, Mom tested the waters by suggesting that Tommy might, when he got off work, join the foursome at the Linger Lounge. He insisted that he would've loved to, but alas, he was otherwise engaged that night. Might he be so bold, he countered, as to ask for her phone number? Indeed he might, she assured him, and she wrote it down on the inside of a Ned's matchbook.

Tommy phoned her the very next night, a Thursday, and they chatted for more than an hour. He asked if she was free to see him on Friday evening, and her first impulse was to say no; after all, how would it look if she agreed to a date on such short notice? She didn't want to give him the idea that she was usually free on a weekend night or that she was willing to be some sort of last resort he could call when all other prospects had proven unavailable.

Still, Tommy seemed awfully sweet and almost naïve, as if he wasn't really aware of the taboo against asking out a woman on such short notice. Mom decided to bend the rules just this once.

He called for her at seven, and they strolled together to the Plaza Theatre, where the fare was a double feature of *Jumping Jacks,* with Jerry Lewis and Dean Martin, and the Bowery Boys in *Here Come the Marines.* The sort of broad comedy served up by those two teams was not really Mom's cup of tea, but Tommy laughed loud and long.

They went out again on Tuesday night, for a few rounds of miniature golf, and again on the following Friday, when Tommy suggested that they might go roller skating, of all things. Mom hadn't set wheeled foot on a roller rink since her freshman year in high school, but she didn't want to seem unadventurous, so she agreed.

The next Wednesday Mom's boss, Mr. Garrett, surprised

Mom by offering her two tickets to that night's performance by the Broadway touring company of *Oklahoma!* She'd never seen a Broadway play, and thrilled at the prospect, she called Tommy to see if he was free to join her.

Tommy regretfully declined, citing a midterm exam that was facing him the following morning. He'd have to stay home and study.

Study? Midterm exam? Mom hadn't even known Tommy was a student. He must be in graduate school, she guessed, or he might even be in his senior year of college. That would make him twenty-two or so, not much younger than she.

But when Mom asked Tommy if he attended Oklahoma City University, which was just a few short blocks from Ned's, he laughed nervously and admitted that, no, he was not enrolled there. He was a senior, but at Northwest Classen, the high school that was directly across the avenue from Ned's. Tommy was, in fact, only seventeen, still a full six weeks away from his eighteenth birthday.

Mom was floored. Never would she have guessed Tommy to be so young. She was now on the horns of a dilemma; she'd grown, in just a few days, inordinately fond of Tommy and was none too keen on ending their fledgling relationship. And so began the inevitable attempts at rationalization: Tommy was in his last semester of high school, she reminded herself; in six short months he'd be a college student, and she was only a year or two out of college herself. And surely relationships between older women and younger men had been made to work before, had they not? Well, in truth, she couldn't come up with any examples of such a successful pairing right off the top of her head, but surely it'd been done. And she told herself that when she was, say, thirty-five, Tommy would be twenty-nine; at that point the difference in their ages wouldn't mean a thing.

These various and sundry rationalizations did the trick for the short term. Mom continued to see Tommy—when he didn't have homework. They'd occasionally take in a Northwest Classen Knights basketball game (Tommy had been the team's trainer the previous season), though they tended to sit far away from Tommy's classmates. As the weather grew warmer, they'd often take in a movie at an area drive-in. Tommy also loved to bowl, an activity at which Mom was not terribly adept; with Tommy's coaching, though, her average score climbed in just a few weeks from 74 to 110.

When May rolled around, Tommy got very busy at school. Long before he and Mom had met, he had volunteered to serve on the commencement committee and had been named chairman of the planning committee for the senior prom as well. He was naturally hesitant to shirk his responsibilities, but Mom couldn't help feeling a bit abandoned. Tommy was apologetic and reminded her that in just a few weeks it'd all be over. He would have graduated, and they would spend a memorable summer together.

But between the pair and that summer of promise stood one treacherous obstacle: the senior prom. Mom was hesitant to attend; she couldn't imagine that she wouldn't feel terribly out of place. But, though she'd never been the jealous type, she also wasn't crazy about the notion that one of Tommy's female classmates might go in her stead, and she didn't think it fair to expect him to go stag or, worse, to miss the prom altogether.

So she agreed to be Tommy's prom date. She took one of her college formals, the yellow organdy one she'd worn only once, down from top shelf in her bedroom closet and made an appointment with Wally, her hairdresser, for that Saturday afternoon.

It wasn't such an unpleasant evening, really—for the first few hours. Tommy looked quite handsome in his tuxedo, and though Mom had never been particularly fond of wrist corsages, the tiny bouquet he slipped over her left hand was quite lovely. Dinner was delicious, although Mom had to instruct Tommy on the finer points of eating lobster, and the dance music at the prom, provided by the Al Good Orchestra, was delightful. Still, holding hands with Tommy amidst several hundred high school students made Mom a little queasy.

After the prom, Mom accompanied Tommy to a party at the home of one of his classmates, where, as is so often the case at such affairs, heavy drinking was the primary activity. A punch-like concoction dubbed Purple Passion and comprising, as far as Mom could tell, grape-flavored Kool-Aid and whatever alcoholic odds and ends the party's young attendees had managed to squirrel away over the last few weeks, was flowing freely. Mom declined to partake, but Tommy plunged right in. Mom had no idea if Tommy had ever done any drinking, but he'd certainly never imbibed in her presence. In fact, she herself hadn't enjoyed a cocktail or a beer since she'd begun seeing Tommy.

In any case, it wasn't long before Tommy was tight, and soon enough the mature front he'd been putting up for so long came tumbling down. He slung his right arm awkwardly around Mom's neck and led her about the premises, alternating between introducing her to his equally tipsy classmates and try-ing (though usually failing) to plant a big, sloppy, purple kiss on her lips.

It wasn't long before Mom had had her fill of that behavior, but she couldn't bring herself to leave the party alone. Mr. Sewell had generously allowed them use of his new Cadillac for the night, and Mom was afraid that if she called a taxi for her-self, Tommy might adjudge himself fit to drive once the party had broken up. So she bore her pie-eyed paramour as long as she could stand it before insisting it was time to go.

If Mom was not already convinced that she and Tommy should call it quits—that at this stage in their lives six years was just too great an interval to be successfully spanned—she cer-tainly was sold on the notion when Tommy, disoriented by the Caddy's rapidly spinning passenger compartment, brought forth a giant purple puddle into her lap. Her lovely yellow or-gandy gown was ruined, and so, once and for all, was a misbe-gotten, if briefly diverting, May-April relationship.

Terry Collins

TERRY Collins has remained a real mystery to Mom. They met in line for tickets to the Stillwater, Oklahoma, premiere of *In the Good Old Summertime* at the Cowboy Theatre downtown. Such a Judy Garland fan was Mom that she arrived an hour and a half before the evening's first show to ensure that she got a ticket, and even so, she was not first in line. Terry had already been waiting for forty-five minutes when Mom arrived.

With time to kill and no one else in line, the two young fans naturally began to chat. Terry, the son of a local jeweler, was one year ahead of Mom in school. He was a biology major and intended to go on to med school, although it became quite clear to Mom that he was not really interested in medicine, that he was only following that path to make his parents happy.

They looked perhaps a bit foolish, the two of them, standing there together waiting for a movie that would not begin for more than an hour. No one else even joined them in line until about fifteen minutes before showtime, just before the box office opened for the evening. But they were so enchanted with each other's company that they scarcely noticed.

Mom suggested that she and Terry sit together, and he readily agreed. As the movie unspooled, Mom, not usually so forward but inspired by Garland's spunky performance, took Terry's hand there in the darkened theatre and didn't let go until the credits had run and the house lights came up.

Thus began a wonderful five-month relationship. Mom and Terry could not, it seemed to all observers, have been happier. They even began to speak of a future together. Terry was, in so many ways, Mom's dream man: a perfect gentleman, a terrific dancer with a wonderful singing voice, a gourmet cook. Their shared interests were many; they liked the same movies, the same music. Without warning, though, Terry left school midway through the spring semester and took off for San Francisco, where he remains to this day. Though he wrote Mom a brief note of apology, he offered no explanation for his sudden departure. They spoke once or twice on the phone, but he seemed so distant somehow that Mom finally gave up and stopped calling.

Today Terry is co-owner of a successful floral-design business that specializes in weddings. Ironically, Terry himself never married.

Gordon Kiley

I F you'd asked Mom on her twenty-second birthday whether later that year she would become involved with a man almost three times her age, she would have laughed in your face. But that's exactly what happened. Mom had just left college, accepting a position as a secretary in Oklahoma City. She scoured the classifieds for an apartment she could afford on her meager salary, and finally decided to take the upstairs in an older home owned by a widower, Gordon Kiley. Mr. Kiley was fifty-nine, an accountant who'd lost his wife of thirty-six years only the year before. He had decided the house was just too quiet without her and so had cleared out the upper floor and placed an ad. Mom was the first person to respond.

It became a habit for the two of them to spend Sunday evenings together; Mom would cook a meal and they would often take a stroll, sometimes stopping for a movie at the Plaza Theatre a few short blocks away. Some evenings they would stay in, though; Gordon would talk about his Emma, and he and

Mom would listen to his Rudy Vallee 78s. Though Mom initially thought of Gordon as sort of a second father, gradually she began to experience deeper feelings for him. One Sunday night, as Rudy Vallee sang, they danced a fox-trot. Without speaking a word, Gordon ever so gently kissed Mom's lips. She returned the kiss but instantly regretted it, feeling something just wasn't right. She feigned a headache and excused herself, retreating to her bedroom upstairs.

The next morning both Gordon and Mom tried to behave as if nothing had happened, but the tension between them was palpable. They continued this way for ten or twelve days, at which point Mom told Gordon she felt she must find another place to live. Within a week, she'd moved out, and two months later Gordon sold the home he'd shared with Emma and moved to Cedar Rapids, Iowa, where his son and daughter-in-law lived. Mom never spoke to Gordon again.

Henry Dixon

I N the summer after her graduation from college, Mom's love life hit an inexplicable and unexpected dry spell. First July and then August came and went with nary a date. She scarcely noticed at first, so busy was she with forging her postcollegiate life in Oklahoma City—landing a satisfying job, finding an apartment she liked, attending various churches until she found one in which she felt at home—but eventually, as things settled down, it occurred to her that somehow her phone was not ringing.

So when Nancy Hoak, a new pal she'd met in the Young Singles Sunday-school class at St. Luke's Methodist Church, asked Mom if she wouldn't consider going on a blind date with Nancy's cousin, Henry Dixon, who was new in town, Mom readily agreed. She'd never been much of one for blind dates— the practice seemed to her a bit like allowing an acquaintance to lay out one's clothes in the morning—but then she'd never really *needed* to pursue this path before. But now, after several weeks of inactivity, she decided that it couldn't hurt, just this once, to trust her new friend's judgment and take a chance on Henry.

When Henry called, he suggested that he and Mom visit the small art center at the state fairgrounds. A traveling exhibition of Cubist art was in town for two weeks, and Henry, who'd spent some years in New York City and had even taken a six-week night class in art appreciation at the New School, relished the opportunity to impress Mom with his expertise. Mom was amenable, and a date was set.

They agreed to meet at the gallery, since Mom thought it a good idea not to depend on Henry for transportation, in case the date proved disastrous. Mom gave a brief description of herself, and Henry agreed to wear a white carnation on his lapel, so that he might be easily spotted if there was a crowd. He needn't have worried.

Mom almost forgot where she was and why she was there upon spying, some hundred yards away, a tallish man—he was perhaps six foot one—in a blue pinstriped suit and a bowler hat making his way across the parking lot. One didn't often see a man wearing a bowler hat in Oklahoma City, but even this odd detail escaped Mom's notice at first. For she could focus on nothing else but this long, lean stranger's humongous nose.

Never had Mom seen such a beezer. It was a snout to make Cyrano count his blessings, a nozzle to render Jimmy Durante's proboscis petite. This was a beak under which one could safely take shelter in case of sudden downpour, a snuffler that could offer shade on a hot summer's day.

And it wasn't long before that schnozz's impressive shadow was cast across Mom's face, for, as you must surely have guessed by now, that nose of noses belonged to Henry; a quick glance at the pale blossom on his lapel confirmed it.

Introductions were exchanged, and the two ducked into the art center. They strolled the gallery for just over an hour, Mom doing her darnedest to resist staring at Henry's nose. But it was no use. To this day she can't explain it, but that darned honker had her hypnotized. Every time Henry turned toward Mom to offer his insights on a particular painting, she'd begin by gazing into his eyes but, despite her best efforts, would soon end up staring at his nose.

Henry was fully aware of her focus, of course, and it wasn't anything he hadn't experienced before, but Nancy had been so enthusiastic about his prospects with Mom, and his first impression of her had been such an encouraging one, that he couldn't help but feel disappointed. If only he could get her to somehow stop staring at his nose.

By the time they'd seen all the paintings, though, Henry had decided that there was little hope. Mom, in a desperate attempt to salvage the afternoon, suggested that they stop off somewhere for a cup of coffee or perhaps an ice cream sundae. But Henry, feeling demoralized, declined.

For two days Mom reproached herself for her lack of self-control. Resolving to somehow make it up to Henry, she invited him to the movies. She hoped that the dimmed theatre lights would solve the problem, but alas, they did not; the reflective glow from the silver screen offered more than sufficient illumination by which to marvel at Henry's mountainous muzzle, and he caught her staring askance on several occasions, despite her best efforts at stealth. Even in the darkened theatre Mom could see the hurt in Henry's eyes.

Mom was distraught. She didn't know whether it would be kinder at this point to throw in the towel or to take one more stab at showing herself less shallow than Henry must certainly have come to think her. The problem was, she didn't see any future for herself with Henry; if it hadn't been for her regrettable behavior, she would definitely have been inclined to cut Henry loose at this point. Unable to bear the thought that he might go through life thinking her insensitive, however, Mom decided to make one last attempt at improving his opinion of her. She felt that if she could manage one full date without getting caught staring, the damage would be sufficiently controlled.

Mom loved zoos and hadn't yet attended the one in Oklahoma City, so she invited Henry to accompany her there the next Sunday afternoon. She wore her darkest sunglasses in the hope that even if she did slip—even if her eyes did stray from the animals to Henry's honker—the dark lenses would keep him from being entirely certain that she was staring at his nose.

But again, fond as she was of the giraffes, lions, and especially the elephants, she simply couldn't control the urge to peek at Henry's own massive trunk. Even with the sunglasses on, Mom was certain that Henry had caught her staring more than once. She began to despair that the situation was unsalvageable, that Henry, himself perfectly pleasant and gentlemanly, would always think of her as a superficial, inconsiderate jerk.

Though it had been sunny for most of the afternoon, a storm began to brew as Mom and Henry neared the end of their zoo tour. Just as they reached the monkey house, the heavens let loose with a deluge. Mom and Henry immediately ran for the parking lot and the shelter of Henry's car, but to no avail. They were both soaked.

Mom saw it as the perfect finish to a rotten day. She was certain that Henry would drive her straight home and she'd never see him again, but to her surprise, he suggested that, despite the soaking, they stop off at the Split T Restaurant for a burger. It was a warm day and Mom was dressed casually in blue jeans and a white cotton blouse, so what harm could a little water do?

It was still pouring when they reached the Split T, and Mom and Henry were both drenched anew as they dashed from the car to the restaurant. Henry selected a booth in the back, and they settled in with menus. Mom knew what she wanted; at the Split T she always ordered the restaurant's specialty—the Theta Burger with a side of fries. But Henry kept his nose buried in the menu as Mom told him an anecdote about a previous visit to the Split T, some months prior, when she'd inadvertently bumped a waiter carrying a huge tray of burgers and beverages, sending the tray and its contents crashing to the floor.

As she spoke, she suddenly realized that Henry's attention was not on the menu at all. Nor was he gazing into Mom's laughing eyes as she told her tale. Instead he was staring at her soaked white cotton blouse as it clung to her body.

Mom cleared her throat rather pointedly, and Henry came out of his lecherous fog. He buried his beet-red face once again in the menu, and Mom continued with her story. Before long, the waiter stopped by, took their order, and retrieved the menus. Henry now had nowhere to hide, and he seemed as powerless to resist staring at Mom's soaked blouse as she had been to avoid looking at his prominent nose. Mom caught him looking no less than three times in the course of the meal, and each time his face grew more crimson. When finally she feigned a chill and asked if she mightn't borrow his sports jacket as a cover-up, he was at once terribly relieved and utterly mortified at having caused her to take such a measure.

Mom couldn't help savoring Henry's discomfort, feeling somehow that their relationship had now taken on a certain equanimity. In a quivering voice, Henry asked if they might not skip dessert just this once, and Mom, taking pity on this man who had, over the last two weeks, inspired in her so many long hours of self-reprobation, acquiesced.

Henry drove a little too fast on the way home and seemed quite relieved when Mom assured him he needn't walk her to the door. That was the last time the pair ever dated, although Mom did see Henry a couple of years later at a Christmas party Nancy threw with her roommate, Helen. Mom was accompanied by my father, to whom she'd been married for some fourteen months, and Henry was in the company of a lovely blonde named Vivian who had, Nancy informed Mom, been named second runner-up in the Miss Oklahoma pageant three years prior. Clearly one woman's Cyrano de Bergerac is another woman's Christian de Neuvillette, as Henry and Viv were wed just eighteen months later. They went on to fill their happy home with Cubist paintings and a half dozen lovely, healthy, big-nosed children.

Micah Westmore

M OM'S very first date, at the age of fourteen, very nearly soured her on the whole business once and for all. His name was Micah Westmore, and he was the son of the new preacher who had arrived to lead Okemah's Pentecostal church only a few weeks before. His father's church was having an open-air potluck supper, and Micah, who, like Mom, was in the eighth grade, asked Mom if she wouldn't like to accompany him. She was somewhat hesitant. She didn't share any classes with Micah and so was somewhat apprehensive about spending the afternoon with a boy she barely knew.

Her parents were apprehensive, too. Her mother felt a bit queasy about the whole affair because Micah was a Pentecostal, and she made no secret of it. She'd always imagined that Mom would eventually settle down with a nice Methodist boy or, at worst, a Presbyterian. Her father didn't see any reason why a fourteen-year-old needed to go on a date, period—with a Methodist, a Presbyterian, a Pentecostal, or a druid.

Still, Mom was taken with the idea of going on her first date, and she managed to convince her parents that her time had come. Granddad called Micah's father and was assured that the potluck supper would be a perfectly tame affair and that he would personally see to it that Mom was well taken care of.

The big day came, and Micah arrived at the front door with a half dozen long-stemmed roses. This gave Granddad pause, and Mom, too. The flowers were lovely, but they seemed a bit much for a first date. However, Micah was a perfect little gentleman and put Granddad, if not Mom, at ease. Grandmother exchanged barely a word with Micah, and just before the two youngsters departed, she pulled Mom aside and informed her in no uncertain terms that if anyone at the supper began to speak in tongues, Mom was to come right home. Mom, rolling her eyes and sighing that sigh reserved by fourteen-year-old girls exclusively for their parents, agreed, and she and Micah were off.

Okemah's a small town, so it was understood that Mom and Micah would walk to the church. It was a beautiful sunny day with a welcome gentle breeze, and Mom was thrilled to be on her very first date. Sure, she'd had some early reservations, and she had been a bit thrown by the roses. But Micah looked very handsome in his black-and-white houndstooth sports jacket and his bow tie of a deep ruby red (it was a clip-on, Mom suspected, though she was too polite to check), and he'd thoughtfully lavished praise on her own outfit, a lovely pink sundress with matching gloves that had been purchased expressly for this event.

But before they'd walked more than a few blocks, Micah had told Mom how pretty she looked at least three more times. The first was appreciated, the second she wrote off to jitters, but the third made her more than a little uncomfortable. Even so, she hadn't minded it when Micah had gently taken her arm and placed it through his own. It made her feel grown-up and sophisticated. Isn't that what people on dates did, after all—walk arm in arm?

Before long, they encountered a young mother pushing an infant in a stroller. After pausing to coo a bit at the child, Micah asked Mom how many children she thought they should have. Mom felt certain she must have misunderstood, but when she asked him to repeat himself, she felt a chill down her back to have it confirmed: He'd asked how many children she thought *they* should have.

Something told Mom to turn and head for home right then and there, but it was Micah's first date, too, and it occurred to her that maybe he was just trying to impress her, that he wanted to appear grown-up. Still, she felt she needed to nip this nonsense in the bud: She'd not given the first thought, she icily informed Micah, to how many children she one day hoped to have, and she certainly hadn't given any consideration to starting a family with him.

Micah tried to shrug it off, as if he'd only been joking, but he admitted that he did think it a good practice for people who know they've found Mr. or Mrs. Right to get married as soon as they're able. His own parents had been only seventeen when they tied the knot, he revealed, and it seemed to have worked out pretty well for them.

Mom was ruing the day she'd agreed to this date, but they were now just two blocks from the church; surely he'd behave once they'd arrived at the potluck supper.

But things only got worse. At the church, Micah introduced her variously as his girl, his steady, his girlfriend—he even presented her to one rather baffled older couple as his fiancée. Mom was mortified and began to look for a way out, but she knew most of the people at the picnic and was hesitant to make a scene.

But when the Reverend Westmore, Micah's father, offered a prayer before the food was served, he inadvertently provided Mom the perfect excuse to flee. The prayer began as a simple blessing of the food they were about to eat, but Reverend Westmore was a robust man of no few words. He moved on from blessing the food to praying for those in need—the hungry, the sick, the indigent—and from there his remarks became less a prayer than a sermon. He asked God to address all the ills and evils—and they were many—that had beset the country: motion pictures, swing music, cigarettes, liquor, gambling, astrology. The litany continued until Miss Steiner, the stern-faced clerk who worked Mondays, Wednesdays, and Fridays in the post office and who, legend had it, had never been seen with a smile on her face, became caught up in Reverend Westmore's fervor and began to utter odd sounds that Mom couldn't quite make out.

Mom had never heard anyone else speak while a minister was praying aloud, and though she kept her head respectfully bowed, she was focused not on Reverend Westmore's exhortations but on the competing proclamations emitting from the far corner of the churchyard. She strained to catch what the postal clerk was saying, and soon it occurred to Mom that it was happening, just as her mother had warned her it might: Miss Steiner was speaking in tongues! Mom was tempted to tarry and listen further, but she couldn't make head or tails of what Miss Steiner was saying, anyway, and here was the perfect excuse to bring her date with the ever-creepier Micah to a sudden close.

Mom whispered in Micah's ear that she had to go and quickly turned to depart. She knew he wouldn't follow her; Reverend Westmore was still praying, and Micah didn't dare walk out on his father mid-prayer.

The following Monday Micah confronted Mom in the hall at school, but when she explained that it was the speaking in tongues that had driven her away, that she'd been following her mother's expressed instructions, Micah knew it would never work out between them. They shook hands and agreed that there would be no hard feelings, and it wasn't long before Micah decided that Mom's best friend, Lois, was the girl for him. Unfortunately for Micah, the natural network that exists among women was his undoing. In no time Lois, and every other female in Okemah, knew that Micah, at the age of fourteen, was actively seeking a wife, and he didn't manage another date in the twenty-six months that his father was assigned to Okemah Pentecostal.

Kathy Simpkins

T HIS would-be suitor was not a man, and Mom never really dated her. Still, the story will be told.

With a few weeks remaining in her junior year of college, Mom decided to enroll in summer school, giving her reason to remain in Stillwater through June, July, and August. The true reason for this decision, however, was that her new beau, Frank, was attending summer school too, and she could spend those warm summer evenings in his company.

Frank pulled a fast one, however, throwing her over for a bleached-blond psych major the night before summer classes were to begin. Mom was devastated, so much so, in fact, that she swore off men for the duration of the summer, vowing not to go out on a date, no matter who might call.

She stuck to her word too. The phone rang often, and Mom spoke with her suitors just long enough so as not to seem un-civil, but the answer was always the same: "I'm sorry, I'm concentrating on my studies this summer and am not interested in going out."

Mom's roommate that summer was an older woman of twenty-five named Kathy Simpkins. Kathy had just begun her studies in American history that spring, after serving a stint in the air force. Mom had responded to an ad Kathy placed in the student paper, seeking someone to share her garage apartment, just off campus, for the summer. Mom and Kathy got along fine—they often cooked dinner together on those summer evenings—but they were not particularly close and Mom had not chosen to share the details of her romantic misfortune with Kathy. In fact, Kathy knew nothing of Mom's romantic or sexual proclivities. All she knew was that every man who called for Mom was firmly, if politely, rebuffed.

It happened after one of those home-cooked meals. Mom and Kathy had gone shopping together that afternoon and splurged on a leg of lamb and a bottle of Beaujolais. Once the dinner was eaten and the plates piled in the kitchen sink, Kathy, emboldened by her third glass of wine, sat right beside Mom on what was rather a large and roomy davenport and, much to Mom's surprise, transformed into an *octopus di amore.*

Mom, caught more than a little off guard, extracted herself from Kathy's clutches, excused herself, and sped off to her bedroom, quickly locking the door behind her.

Interactions between Mom and Kathy were, quite naturally, a little awkward for a day or two afterward, with only a few words exchanged between them. Eventually, though, they sat down and talked things over. Mom explained that her moratorium on men was a temporary one, and Kathy apologized for her aggressive behavior. The rest of the summer went by without incident.

Today Kathy resides in Grand Rapids, Michigan, where she enjoyed a long career as a high school history teacher. She retired only last year. She and Mom still exchange Christmas cards.

Roger Fleming

Roger Fleming is one man my mother *didn't* date. But it wasn't for lack of effort on her part. Mom was usually pretty levelheaded in her romantic dealings, but everyone is occasionally a fool for love and Roger brought out the fool in Mom.

They met during Mom's sophomore year in college. Roger was a junior majoring in agricultural sciences, a field of study in which Oklahoma A&M was a standout.

On the first day of the fall semester, Mom entered the cavernous Williams Hall classroom where her "American History: 1865 to the Present" class would meet every Monday, Wednesday, and Friday for the next four and a half months. Looking for a friend or acquaintance with whom to sit, Mom didn't spy a single familiar face among the hundred or more people seated in the classroom. So she turned instead to Plan B: Who in the room might she *want* to get to know?

This was an easy decision. There was a lad sitting off to one side all by his lonesome who immediately rang the "Dreamboat" bell on Mom's Male-o-Meter. He was long and lean—six foot three if he was an inch, and he couldn't have weighed more than 190 pounds. His hair was russet, his eyes deep blue; his face was dappled with a sprinkling of freckles that suggested a man who spends long hours out of doors, and yet the elements had not yet begun to erode his features but had instead given him a burnished ruddiness that was quite appealing.

Mom marched right over and sat in the seat in front of his. Perhaps he also knew no one in the class, she thought to herself. Surely he'd greet this fresh-faced beauty when she made the rather obvious gesture of joining him in no man's land, yes?

No. Roger didn't say hello that first day or the following Wednesday or on that Friday, either. He always sat alone, and though Mom was not so obvious as to sit right in front of him every time, she was never more than a few seats away. He never gave her the time of day.

Mom refused to be thrown by the fact that Roger was a bit on the diffident side; she decided it was an endearing trait. On Monday of the second week, she again planted herself right in front of him, turned around, gave him her most engaging smile, introduced herself, and asked him his name and what he'd thought of that weekend's assigned reading on the Reconstruction. He was civil enough but not terribly forthcoming. His name was Roger, he told her, and he'd only finished the reading a few minutes prior to leaving for class, so he'd really not had time to consider the material very carefully.

Mom was less than thrilled with this first encounter, but she tried to put a positive face on it. She'd at least broken the ice; she knew his name and he knew hers. Surely he would warm up soon. As class let out, she made a point of saying good-bye to Roger, but he gave her only a barely discernible nod in return.

Mom refused to feel discouraged. She'd dealt with shy men before, and she had no doubt that, if she put her mind to it, she'd bring Roger out of his shell. And put her mind to it she did. By sheer force of will, over the next few weeks, she pried the following snippets of information out of him: He was unattached. His family lived just northwest of Ponca City, Oklahoma. His father was a farmer, and it was Roger's intention, after graduation, to return to the family farm and—when his father was ready to retire—to buy it and run it as his own. Roger rarely asked Mom anything about herself, though she volunteered that she, too, was single, that she was from Okemah but had always dreamed of living on a farm (this was patently untrue), and that strawberry was her favorite flavor of ice cream. She'd shared this last tidbit because there was an ice cream social at the student union one Monday night to which she'd hoped Roger might invite her, but he somehow resisted the temptation. He also resisted, on successive weekends and despite a string of rather blatant hints, inviting Mom to the football homecoming dance, the school play (*The Man Who Came to Dinner*), and a double feature of *Blondie Hits the Jackpot* and *Blondie's Big Deal* at the Cowboy Theatre.

Mom was at the end of her rope. She found herself thinking of this man, who was still all but a complete stranger, day and night. Some evenings she'd call him two and three times, just to hear his voice—pretending, in a series of put-on voices, to have reached a wrong number. She'd seen actors in movies place a handkerchief over the phone receiver in an effort to avoid being recognized, so she adopted the same approach, though she doubted it really helped.

Mom soon began to drive by Roger's apartment almost nightly, just to see if lights were shining in his window. She even took to sitting in the tiny park across the street from his building to watch his comings and goings. Most nights he neither came nor went, but that didn't stop her; she fully intended to be there if he did venture out. But would she speak to him? Pretend to be just passing by—visiting a sick friend, perhaps? Would she exclaim, "Why, Roger Fleming, imagine bumping into you, of all people!"? She didn't really know what she'd do if he appeared, and it never came up. Once he did appear, but that was only to drop a letter in the corner mailbox just two doors away. He was in and out in less than two minutes, and Mom's heart was in her throat the entire time.

Mom's fever finally broke, along with her fibula, one night in early November. She'd resorted to climbing the mimosa tree that grew outside Roger's second-floor apartment window in an attempt to catch a glimpse of him at home. She wondered what his apartment looked like, what he ate, what he drank. How did he pass the time? Did he listen to the radio? Read? Play solitaire?

Roger had just left his living room, which Mom could clearly see from her perch, and entered his bedroom, which she could not, when the branch on which Mom was standing snapped in two, sending her plummeting to the ground. At first she thought only her pride had been hurt, but as she struggled to limp her way back to her dorm room, she feared she'd done serious damage to her left leg in the fall. A visit to the emergency room confirmed it: She had a hairline fracture of the fibula and would be in a cast and on crutches for several weeks. Mom's stalking days were over.

Mom didn't lack for offers from interested men to carry her books to class, but she made a habit of sitting in the very last row, so as not to have to struggle down the aisle on crutches any further than necessary. As a result, her contact with Roger was now more limited than ever. He did deign, however—per her request—to sign her cast, and when finally the cast came off, Mom urged the doctor to wield his saw with care so as to preserve Roger's signature. That piece of plaster now rests in my parents' attic, in a shoe box filled with ticket stubs, pressed corsages, and other college souvenirs and mementos.

By December, Roger decided that a degree was not necessary for a successful career in farming, so he never returned for the spring semester. Word has it he retired in 1994, turning the operation of the family farm over to his own son; Mom's had no contact with Roger since she wished him a Merry Christmas on the last day of the fall semester of her sophomore year.

Robert "Slim" Matthews

ROBERT "SLIM" MATTHEWS was widely regarded as the most attractive boy at Okemah High. He made good grades and treated Mom like a queen on their lone date (a milkshake at the Dairy Boy and the football homecoming game against Wewoka High). So what was the problem? Slim was studying to be a welder, and Mom's mom forbade her dating him again, saying, "We're just not vo-tech people." Slim, who never married, owns three welding shops in San Antonio and dances a single fox-trot with Mom every five years at their class reunion.

Martin Tamblyn

MOM spent much of the summer after her sophomore year in high school with grease under her fingernails and motor oil in her hair.

That was the year that Martin Tamblyn spent June, July, and August helping out on his grandparents' pecan orchard a few miles west of Okemah. His grandfather had had back surgery and naturally wasn't up to his usual workload, so Martin, who lived in St. Louis, came down to help out until his Pa-pa was back on his feet.

Mom met Marty early one June evening at the Phillips 66 station on the western edge of town. She'd stopped in for a pack of Beeman's gum; he was there to purchase a set of spark plugs. As she entered the station, she noticed a stranger deep in conversation with Sam, the weekend-night man who was a maintenance worker at the high school during the week. Marty was blue-eyed, skinny, and just a bit taller than Mom at five foot eight. Several times in the course of the conversation, he referred, with evident fondness, to someone by the name of Ida, leading Mom to ruefully conclude that this attractive newcomer was already spoken for. But when Marty mentioned that Ida was due for a lube job—Ida, as it turned out, was Marty's souped-up 1938 Ford coupe—Mom went to work.

She introduced herself to Marty and asked if he wasn't new in town. He explained that he'd only arrived two days earlier. He pointedly mentioned that he'd never before been to Okemah—his grandparents, it seems, had long made it a habit to visit their daughter and her family in St. Louis twice each year—and so he knew no one in town. That didn't last long.

Within the hour, Mom and Marty were seated in the back booth at the Dairy Boy on Cherry Street, sharing a banana split and their respective life stories. The next night, an unseasonably cool one, found them snuggled up in Ida's front seat at the Okemah Drive-in, ignoring a double feature of *Devil Monster* and *Valley of the Zombies.* Mom's social calendar for the summer was, it appeared, set.

Running the pecan orchard was hard work, though, and it left Marty with little time for romance. Every minute that he wasn't working the rows and rows of pecan trees, Marty devoted to Ida. So Mom figured that if she couldn't beat 'em, she'd join 'em. Most nights that summer found her sprawled on the grass, watching for falling stars, as a few feet away Marty leaned under Ida's open hood, tools in hand, tweaking, tuning, and tightening.

But every now and then, late on a moonlit night, Marty and Mom would take Ida out on some deserted county road and let 'er rip. On a couple of occasions Marty even slid over to the passenger seat and let Mom take the wheel. She loved to rev the engine, savoring the force of Ida's powerful V8, and once she'd popped the clutch and put her in motion, she'd floor the gas pedal and take Ida up over a hundred miles per hour.

In St. Louis Marty was the president of the area hot-rod club. The group had made arrangements with a local drag strip to hold monthly meets, which, because they were supervised by the police department, made the local authorities very happy. At least Marty and his fellow car enthusiasts weren't racing one another in the streets.

Okemah, though, was a tiny town of only a few thousand and had no such arrangement. In fact, very few Okemah boys even owned a car, much less a hot rod, so there was no local competition for Marty and his Ida.

However, in Henryetta, a community of some twenty thousand residents a half hour east of Okemah, there lived a speed demon by the name of Tal Gossage. Gossage caught wind that there was a new hot-rodder in the vicinity, and having long since vanquished all competition in Henryetta, he decided he'd take a little drive over Okemah way.

Aside from their shared interest in fast cars, Tal and Marty couldn't have been more different. Marty was a straight-A student who planned to go to law school. Tal, who was four years Marty's elder, was a dropout who'd spent more time in reform school than he had in the classroom and was on the troublemaker list of every law-enforcement officer in Okfuskee County.

So when Tal tracked down Marty one Saturday night at the Dairy Boy, where Marty and Mom were sharing their traditional banana split, he walked up to their booth and loudly

challenged Marty, right there in front of the several dozen people who'd packed the restaurant that night, to a race the length
of Lakeside Lane, the half-mile, two-lane road that led from
County Line Road to Lake Okemah a few miles northeast of
town. Having thus thrown down the gauntlet, he added insult
to injury by leaning over, whispering something overtly sugges-
tive in Mom's ear, and planting a kiss right on her mouth. He
then turned on his heel and strolled confidently out the door as
the room sat in stunned silence.

At first Marty just shrugged the matter off, but Tal made almost daily pilgrimages west from Henryetta to Okemah,
spreading the rumor that Marty was chicken, that he'd never
won a race in his life, that he was all talk and no action. Marty
wasn't bothered by the fuss; he was only in Okemah for the
summer, after all, and didn't really care if his reputation in the
town was tarnished.

But Mom was, quite naturally, torn; she tried to adopt
Marty's nonchalant attitude, but it wasn't easy. After all, no girl
wanted to see her boyfriend tarred with the coward's brush.
Okemah was her hometown, and she'd be forced to listen to the
whispers long after Marty had returned to St. Louis. And she
could still feel Tal's fetid breath on her neck as he'd loomed over
her that night. She admired Marty's easygoing manner, on the
one hand, but she couldn't help but wonder if the best approach
wouldn't be to accept Tal's challenge and blow that loud-
mouthed lout's doors off. Over the next few days, Mom urged
Marty to reconsider. She just knew that he and Ida could take
Tal, she insisted repeatedly, and in doing so, he would not only

be defending his own reputation but her honor and the very standing in the region of the town of Okemah itself.

Marty finally agreed, if somewhat reluctantly, to accept Tal's challenge. But he insisted that the race be kept a secret, with only two witnesses on hand—Tal's girlfriend, Joetta, would start the race, and Mom would stand at the finish line to confirm the winner. Tal was now so feverish for the thrill of competition that he readily assented to Marty's terms. They agreed to meet at midnight the following Sunday, when there would be no one at the lake.

A discerning reader could be excused, at this point in the story, for objecting to my depiction of Marty; surely, one might reasonably insist, he could not have been as perfect as this telling of the tale has thus far painted him. And you'd be absolutely correct in guessing him to be not unflawed. After all, every Achilles has his heel, and Marty's was his nose. After several weeks in the hot, dry air of an Oklahoma summer, he had recently proven extremely prone to nosebleeds. St. Louis summers were scarcely cooler, but the air there was so heavy with humidity that nothing dried out, least of all Marty's nasal passages.

At 11:40 on that moonless August night, Marty and Mom, after an evening of church and cheeseburgers, pointed Ida toward Lake Okemah and Marty's date with destiny. Mom couldn't have been prouder of her Marty than she felt that night, and she was certain that he would easily defeat Tal, thereby restoring order to their lives. So pleased was she with her knight in shining chrome and cherry-red paint that she allowed herself for the first time to imagine that, though they'd be faced with a long-distance relationship for at least two years, perhaps she and Marty might actually have a future together. She had just begun to imagine herself some seven years down the road, working to support Marty (and—dare she dream it?—a toddler or two) while he attended law school, when she dreamily gazed over at her handsome Sir Galahad, only to bolt upright and gasp audibly upon spying a tiny crimson spot on his bleached white T-shirt.

Marty was having a nosebleed.

It was only a small one at present, but when Marty's nose began to bleed, a trickle generally gave over pretty quickly to a heavy scarlet flow, leaving Marty no alternative but to lie with his head back until the flood had receded.

Mom had Marty pull over so she could think a moment. They switched seats so that he could tilt his head back, holding Mom's favorite embroidered hankie to his nose; Mom, meanwhile, took the wheel and continued toward Lake Okemah.

As it happened, Mom was wearing a pink summer sweater over her sleeveless white cotton blouse. When she recalled that she had a head scarf in her purse, she began to see a way out of their dilemma. She tucked her ponytail up under the Okemah Panthers baseball cap that Marty had taken to wearing that summer and ordered him to remove his Levi's jacket. Against his heated protests, she insisted that he don her sweater and cover his crew cut with her scarf. If Mom was to have anything to say about it, Ida was going to make Tal eat his words tonight, even if Marty couldn't be at her wheel.

A few minutes later, they were turning off the county road and onto Lakeside Lane. They motored down to the sharp right turn that kept the road from plunging into the lake, where Tal and Joetta were waiting. Tal started right in, razzing Marty for showing up late (he and Mom, in fact, had arrived three or four minutes after the appointed hour of midnight); from inside Ida's sheltering darkness, Marty cut short Tal's diatribe, telling him to stow it and start his blasted car.

Once Tal had turned his Olds Rocket 88 back toward the entrance to Lakeside Lane, where the race would begin, Marty, in Mom's pink sweater and head scarf and with her handkerchief pressed firmly to his nose, emerged from Ida's passenger door and remained at the finish line as Mom made a U-turn, pointing Ida slowly back the way they had come.

As Mom reached the starting line, Tal was revving his engine threateningly. Once she'd maneuvered Ida into position alongside Tal's car and to his left, Joetta, whose father was the track coach at Henryetta High, stood between the two cars, pointed skyward the starter's pistol she'd taken from her father's drawer, and asked if both drivers were ready. Tal bellowed, "You'd better believe it!" Mom, who, of course, could not speak without giving herself away, just revved Ida's engine. Joetta announced that she would count to three and then fire the pistol, at which point the race was on.

And so she did. At the sound of the shot, Mom let up on the clutch and hit the gas pedal. She was a bit slower out of the gate than Tal, but she tried to forget about him, endeavoring instead to keep her eyes on the finish line and to concentrate on

smoothly shifting gears. So focused was she that she almost forgot Tal's car was beside her. It wasn't long before she'd made up
the ground that he'd gained from her sluggish start and started
to pull away from Tal. When they reached the finish line, Mom
and Ida were nearly a full car length ahead. Mom quickly took
the car out of gear and rode the brakes, coming to a stop just as
she reached the sharp right turn in the road.

Tal, who had watched in disbelief as Marty (or so he thought)
and Ida had pulled away, was so intent on trying to close the gap
during the last few seconds of the race that he forgot about the
sharp right turn, and before he knew it, the lake loomed before
him. Though he slammed on his brakes just as he left the road, it
wasn't enough—soon the front end of his Rocket 88 was in four
feet of water and embedded so deeply in the mud of Lake
Okemah that a tow truck was required to free it.

Tal was, of course, beside himself when he learned that not
only had he lost, he'd been beaten by a danged girl! He thought
of protesting, of declaring the results of the race null and void,
but once he had calmed down, he realized that if he couldn't
beat Ida with an inexperienced driver like Mom at the wheel,
what chance did he have of taking her when Marty was driving?
Besides, he hoped that if he clammed up about the whole affair,
maybe word wouldn't spread that he'd lost to a dame.

Tal looked so pale with disappointment and embarrassment
that Mom almost felt sorry for him. She and Marty agreed not
to reveal that Mom had beaten Tal if he would agree to return to
Okemah in the coming days and spread the word that Marty
had beaten him fair and square. Tal readily assented, and he
lived up to his end of the bargain. The following Saturday night

found him at the Dairy Boy, raising his root beer float in a toast to Marty and his Ida and proclaiming himself defeated in fair-and-square fashion.

Soon thereafter, Marty and Ida returned to St. Louis. He and Mom corresponded briefly, but in the end their affair went the way of most summer romances. By October, Mom was fully back in the swing of things, dating-wise, and Marty was again devoting all his free time to Ida.

Vince Skankly

T H E summer after her junior year in high school, Mom met a man who led her on an exciting, if frightening, adventure. His name was Vince Skankly. He was the knife thrower in a small regional circus called Blitzstein Brothers.

The Blitzstein Brothers had a three-day stand in Okmulgee, just a short drive from Mom's hometown of Okemah. A circus in a neighboring burg was a rare treat indeed, and Mom, accompanied by her friend Lois, attended each of the troupe's four performances.

It was after the Saturday matinée that she met Vince. He was standing near the performer's entrance to the lone Blitzstein Brothers tent, smoking a Lucky Strike. Darkly handsome and quite a bit older than Mom, he had a worldly quality about him. He seemed cut of different cloth than any male she'd ever encountered in Okemah.

They chatted a few minutes, and just before she left, he asked her to meet him following that evening's performance at the coffee shop in the town square, just a few blocks away. Mom, surprising herself, agreed.

Over several cups of joe, Vince regaled Mom with tales of the places he'd been, the things he'd seen. Blitzstein Brothers toured four states—Oklahoma, Kansas, Arkansas, and Missouri—so Vince had been as far as Kansas City and St. Louis, towns Mom had only dreamed of seeing. He had been married once, briefly, and had even spent some time in Mexico with a traveling carnival.

Mom was enraptured, swept away by this man. As they stepped outside the café, Vince revealed that his assistant, Zora, was leaving him after the next day's matinée. Taking Mom in his arms and kissing her, he implored her to come with him on the road and be his partner. Mom agreed. They decided she would meet him the following weekend in Tulsa, where the Blitzstein Brothers were next booked.

To make her escape, Mom told her parents that she and Lois were taking the bus to Tulsa for an overnight shopping excursion, that they would be staying with Lois's aunt Cathy there and would return on Saturday evening. This would give her a head start, twenty-four hours during which she would not be missed.

Vince met her at the bus station and took her to the room he'd booked, for the duration of the circus's two weeks in Tulsa, at a downtown boardinghouse. He carried with him, while on the road, a fold-up corkboard, which he used to keep his throwing skills finely honed, and he wanted to get in a little rehearsal time with Mom before that evening's performance.

As Mom stood with her back to the cork, facing this man she hardly knew as he took aim with his knife, her knees began to shake. Before she had time to protest, however, the first blade whizzed through the air toward her. It stuck in the cork firmly, just above her head. A second followed shortly thereafter, firmly imbedding itself in the corkboard just an inch or two away from her left shoulder. When finally she felt the cold steel of the third blade just above her right elbow, she knew she'd made a horrible mistake. She screamed at Vince to stop and stepped quickly away from the corkboard. The cut on her arm was a small one, but it bled profusely and Mom was trembling.

Mom immediately called Lois at her aunt's number; Lois and Cathy came right over and retrieved Mom, taking her back to Cathy's efficiency apartment to tend the wound. Mom's parents were never the wiser, as she and Lois returned to Okemah that Saturday evening as promised. Two weeks of long sleeves ensured that the knife wound was not discovered. Mom never had contact with Vince again.

Sela Mohammed Brouley

WHILE Mom was a junior in college, Oklahoma A&M launched a campaign to attract more foreign students to the university. Since the school was renowned for its excellence in the fields of animal husbandry and the agricultural sciences, the effort proved a notable success; students from all over the world began to flock to Stillwater, in numbers that caught the administration a bit off guard.

A sort of mentoring program was established wherein local students would take two or three foreign students under their wing, to introduce them to American customs and help them negotiate this strange new culture. Mom, who'd never been out of the country—in fact hadn't been east of Tulsa, west of Albuquerque, south of El Paso, or north of Wichita—signed up for the program and was assigned two foreign students: Martha Eckels, a young British woman from just outside of London, and Sela Mohammed Brouley, a young man from the Ivory Coast.

Martha had leapt at the chance to attend school in the United States but only because it allowed her the opportunity to escape the watchful gaze of her overprotective parents. Not a terribly serious student, she seemed to focus primarily on enjoying A&M's social scene, and in this arena she required no guidance. A lithe beauty with a fetching accent, she was swept up in the social whirlpool immediately and had only signed up for the mentoring program because it was required of all exchange students; after two or three brief lunches she stopped returning Mom's calls altogether.

Sela was another matter. Although his English was better than he seemed to realize, he was never entirely comfortable speaking it, much preferring the French of his native land. His skin color also made him feel terribly out of place. Not that anyone was openly rude to him, but there were only a small handful of Negro students on campus and none spoke French. Sela soon found that he was unbearably homesick and desperately lonely. He and Mom made a habit of lunching weekly in the student-union cafeteria; she'd answer any questions he might have about the workings of the university and the quirks of American culture. But more important, she seemed willing to listen as he reminisced about the life he'd left behind.

Sela had only come to the United States to appease his father, a coffee farmer intent upon passing on the family business to Sela, his eldest son. In fact, the elder Brouley had mapped out, as was the tradition, his son's entire future; not only was he making arrangements for Sela to take over the farm, he'd already selected for his son a bride, whom Sela was to wed upon his return home after completing his studies. His bride-to-be,

Azara, was the daughter of a successful cocoa-plantation owner, and their nuptials, then still two years away, were already eagerly anticipated in the region surrounding Sela's father's farm.

Never would Sela have thought to question the path his father had assigned him. It was the traditional way, the way things had been done for generations, even centuries. So it was with a mix of exhilaration and dread that he found himself experiencing deeper feelings for Mom. Not only was he promised to another, but Sela had noticed that A&M's Negro students tended to keep to themselves. There seemed to be little, if any, mingling of the races in social settings and no interracial dating whatsoever.

For her part, the only male Negro Mom had ever known before meeting Sela was Henry Johnson, a janitor at Okemah High. Mom's father, Okemah's superintendent of schools, hosted an annual holiday reception to honor his employees, so Henry, who lived in nearby Boley, a tiny Negro town just twelve miles west of Okemah, had been a guest in her parents' home for several Decembers running. But he was a shy, retiring man, and he'd said little to her over the years beyond "Hello, Miss Karen. How nice to see you today. Happy holidays to you."

But now she and Sela were growing ever closer, and while she was pleased that this sad, lonely, displaced young man was turning to her for the sort of closeness and companionship his life so sorely lacked, she had good reason to fear the reaction of her fellow students and the townspeople of Stillwater to this evolving relationship.

One November afternoon, following their weekly Friday lunch, Sela offered to walk Mom to her nineteenth-century English literature class. The campus was not as crowded as usual that day; many students were skipping classes that afternoon in hopes of getting an early start on their weekend.

But someone was watching when Sela slipped his hand into Mom's, and it soon became clear that the observer, whoever it was, disapproved. It was just a brief hand-in-hand stroll across campus, the most innocent of physical overtures, but it was enough to inspire a firestorm of violence and vandalism. By six-thirty that evening, when Sela, having attended his own Friday-afternoon classes, returned to his rented garage apartment two blocks from campus, someone had spray-painted the words NIGGER GO HOME on his door. Once Sela had locked himself safely inside the apartment, the phone rang ten times in the course of an hour, each call bringing a string of hateful epithets and threats. And when a brick came crashing through his bed-room window at eleven-fifteen that night, Sela was thrown into a panic.

Not knowing what to do, he called Mom, who immediately phoned the Stillwater police on his behalf before rushing over to his apartment. A squad car was dispatched to take the pair to the stationhouse, where they patiently answered each of the de-tectives' myriad questions. For his own protection, Sela spent that night in a jail cell, while Mom slept at the apartment of her close friend Barbara Gillespie.

Saturday night found Mom in her own bed and Sela back in his apartment, a Stillwater police officer stationed at his front door. There were no further incidents, but Sela was incon-solable. He felt he'd foolishly placed Mom at risk, and he feared for his own safety. On Sunday he wired his father that he would be returning home; on Monday he withdrew from the university; and by Tuesday noon he was on the bus to Oklahoma City, where he would board a plane to New York City and travel on to the Ivory Coast.

A month later Mom received a letter in Sela's tidy, carefully crafted handwriting apologizing for the trouble he'd caused and thanking her for the kindness and courage she'd shown him. Mom still has that letter, though it's barely legible in those spots where her tears fell the first time she read it.

Today Sela and Azara are happy and prosperous, the parents of five grown sons, the eldest of whom, some ten years ago, married a woman of his parents' choosing. He is now poised to take over the farm so carefully tended by his father, his father's father, and his father before him.

Nelson Filmont

 MOM was, as we've established, never lacking in suitors, but none were as attractive as Nelson Filmont, a theatre major who transferred to Oklahoma A&M from Southern Methodist University during her junior year. Even Mom herself was not as pretty as Nelson. His was the kind of masculine pulchritude that turned heads as he walked across campus. Some of those enrapt coeds thought Nelson resembled Tyrone Power; others said Robert Taylor. But they all agreed on one thing: Nelson Filmont was the best-looking man on campus, in the town of Stillwater, perhaps even in the entire state of Oklahoma. He was, in short, dreamy.

Mom wasn't usually drawn to pretty boys, but even she was not immune to Nelson's charms. And when he slid one autumn evening into the last empty seat in a third-floor reading room at the library—the chair directly across the table from the one in which Mom was sitting—she couldn't believe her good fortune. Perhaps he'd been waiting for that particular chair to be vacated, she thought to herself, her imagination running away with her. Maybe he'd had his eye on Mom for weeks but had been too shy to speak to her. And now here she sat, not three feet away from him. Surely he'd introduce himself, make small talk, ask about her major, anything that might break the ice. But no—for more than two hours, they sat tantalizingly close and only once did he speak, and that was to ask Mom to please stop tapping her pencil on the smooth surface of the old wooden table.

Mom was mortified. She'd managed only to annoy Nelson, not attract him. Why had she waited for him to speak? There was no reason in the world that a young woman couldn't speak to a young man. Was there?

That squandered opportunity haunted Mom, and she resolved to overcome the bad start she'd made with Nelson. A&M's was a relatively small campus, and Mom often spotted her prey on the way to and from class. When she did, she made it a practice to cross his path. Each time she encountered him in this fashion, she flashed her warmest smile. Eventually she began to sense in his gaze the twinkle of recognition and, yes, even interest.

It was in that same library reading room that she finally broke through; she spotted Nelson with his nose buried in a leather-bound edition of *Romeo and Juliet* and rushed over to capture the seat next to his, managing to slide into that overstuffed leather armchair just ahead of a precocious freshman coed who had thought, mistakenly, that surely her own ship had come in, that she would finally get the chance to chat up the widely adored Nelson Filmont.

It was as he turned the page to Act II, Scene III that Nelson finally looked up and noticed Mom sitting there. Her face now familiar (though he was not entirely sure why), he said hello. She responded warmly and the trap snapped shut. Romeo and his Juliet would have to wait for another night; for the duration of this evening, Nelson Filmont's attentions were spoken for.

Of course Nelson asked Mom out for a late-night burger and cherry Coke when the library closed down for the night. And of course she said yes. Quite naturally he offered to walk her to her dorm afterward, and it being so late, she did not think of declining. The very next night he took her to see Humphrey Bogart (his favorite actor) and Eleanor Parker in *Chain Lightning,* and that was that: The two were an item. As word of the pairing spread, Mom became the envy of every girl on campus.

Through the ages, sages have counseled us to be careful for what we wish, lest our wishes be granted. As Mom was soon to learn, never was a truism truer. Mom had her man, but she soon found that keeping him played havoc with her nerves. Nelson may have been spoken for, but few of the women on campus were content, it seemed, to take this setback lying down. Wherever she and Nelson went—to a party, say, or the soda fountain at the student union or even Sunday-morning services at the Methodist church—Mom could no more than turn her back— to visit the ladies' room or to quench her thirst at a water fountain—without some blonde, brunette, or redhead swooping in to make time with Nelson. Even men seemed oddly drawn to her date, inflicting upon Mom perhaps the deepest of wounds. Having to compete with her beau for the attention of other men was certainly not something to which she was accustomed.

The whole state of affairs was exasperating; Mom grew increasingly resentful at all the attention Nelson received. After all, she wasn't so bad-looking herself; why must Nelson be the center of attention all the time?

The situation came to a head in early November when Republic Pictures launched a regional promotion—in Texas, Oklahoma, and Kansas—to select a man to be named "the New Face of 1951." The lucky winner would receive a trip to Hollywood and a screen test that would be viewed by the bigwigs at Republic. Stillwater was to host one of these beefcake buffets, and Nelson, who'd long dreamed of Hollywood stardom, naturally rushed to sign up. Mom—certain that Nelson would handily win the local competition and fearful that he'd sweep the statewide and regional contests as well—responded by doing something she'd never before considered: She entered a beauty pageant. She couldn't explain her actions, but somehow she'd come to so resent Nelson's good looks, and all the fuss they fostered, that she was now rather desperately seeking reassurance regarding her own appeal.

Though not a classic beauty, Mom did possess a wholesome girl-next-door quality, a warm smile, a winning manner, and an innovative, if not quite daring, sense of personal style. Still, while these are all traits that serve one well in daily life, they seldom suffice in the cutthroat world of beauty competitions. Mom had entered an arena for which she was not properly armed.

The Miss Stillwater contest was held the very same night as the New Face of 1951 competition. Mom—who, for the talent portion of the competition, played "Heart and Soul" on the piano—came in a disappointing ninth out of ten contestants;

she was given the Miss Congeniality award, but that did little to stabilize her teetering self-image. Nelson, of course, walked away with the top prize at the local New Face of 1951 competition and easily won at the statewide and regional levels, too, just as Mom feared he would.

By December, Nelson was in Hollywood and Mom was again dating around. Nelson's screen test was disastrous, but he didn't let that stop him. He set about making the rounds of agents, casting directors, and managers. Eventually he managed to snag an uncredited role as a pirate in *Abbott and Costello Meet Captain Kidd.* He also worked as an extra in *It Grows on Trees* and in *Battle Circus,* a single day's work that gave him the opportunity to meet his idol, Humphrey Bogart, who was, alas, hungover and refused to sign an autograph.

By 1954, however, Nelson was working full-time as the night manager of a twenty-four-hour pancake restaurant in Pasadena, and Mom was engaged to marry my father. Today Nelson is the co-owner of a movie-memorabilia shop on Hollywood Boulevard.

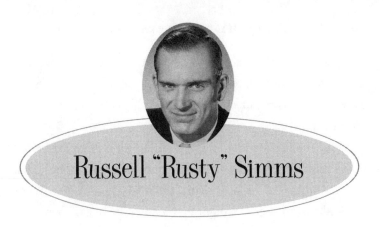

Russell "Rusty" Simms

MOM returned from the Thanksgiving break of her senior year in college to learn that three of her closest friends had become engaged over the four-day weekend. While Mom was pleased for them, she felt a bit left out. It wasn't that she wasn't dating—she was, and often, but they were friendly dates, a movie, perhaps, or a soda at the student union with the same boys she'd been seeing off and on throughout her seven semesters at school.

She found herself craving the sense of security and commitment her friends now had. After all, graduation was just one short semester away. Wasn't it time she began to think of her future, to actively seek a life partner?

Opportunity came knocking at the annual Christmas Ball. Though Mom was escorted by Gil Russert, one of her standbys, she spent a good portion of the evening in the company of Russell "Rusty" Simms. Rusty, recently returned to the States from a stint in the army and a brief tour of duty in South Korea, was the older brother of a classmate. A big man, at six foot two and 260 pounds, and quite dashing in his uniform, he pursued Mom with fervor, and she allowed herself to be swept up in his enthusiasm.

Mom and Rusty spent four straight evenings together before Christmas break, and he called her nightly during the holidays. He even surprised her by showing up at 5:00 P.M. on New Year's Eve and treating her to a night on the town in Tulsa, where they feasted on lobster Newburg and champagne, swinging and swaying the night away to the sounds of the Sammy Kaye Orchestra. At midnight Rusty presented Mom with a beautiful diamond ring and a proposal of marriage. Caught up in the excitement of the moment, emboldened by the champagne, Mom said yes.

As the big day drew near, Mom began to doubt her decision to marry Rusty. Those little quirks unique to her betrothed began to seem off-putting: the loud ties he favored, the way he answered the telephone ("*Yello*"), the fact that he managed a pet store and carried on him the intermingled scents of cat litter, fish food, and dog hair.

In the end she decided that the envy she'd felt of her newly engaged friends had clouded her judgment. She broke the engagement just nine days before the wedding was to have taken place. Naturally, Rusty was crushed, and upon realizing that Mom was resolute in her decision, he moved to Montreal, where he owns a chain of discount pet stores. He has been married three times.

The Eddie Cantor Six

I n the summer of 1953 Mom attended, in a period of two weeks, six different screenings of *The Eddie Cantor Story* at the Plaza Theatre in Oklahoma City, each with a different man.

The first, on a Monday evening, was in the company of Hubert Flanders. Hubert was a dentist who had trouble leaving his work at the office. He insisted on rehashing the various procedures he'd performed that day for Mom's benefit. This first viewing of the movie was her eighth date with Hubert, and her last. She broke it off with him as he walked her home.

The very next day, Mickey Calvinetti, a co-worker at Garrett Grommett Corp., stopped by Mom's desk. Mickey had been after Mom for a date for some time and was delighted to oblige when Mom suggested that they go out that very evening. He took her to a restaurant owned by his uncle Vito. After a delightful veal piccata, he suggested they take in a movie. After all, the Plaza was just a few blocks away and he'd heard great things about this new Eddie Cantor biopic.

On Friday morning, Mom was asked out by Smitty, her milk-man. He inquired offhandedly after her weekend plans and she admitted that she hadn't any. Smitty, who'd long admired Mom but feared attempting to bridge the chasm that exists between milkman and client, finally took the plunge. Mom agreed but cringed inwardly when Smitty spoke of his desire to take in *The Eddie Cantor Story.* He'd seemed so shy and apprehensive about ask-ing her out, though, that she feared she'd scare him off if she hedged. She had, after all, no desire to spend her Friday night at home alone.

Early Sunday evening Mom attended a gathering of young singles at St. Luke's Methodist Church. As the gath-ering broke up, Lloyd Leveridge, on whom Mom had long had her eye, asked if she wouldn't like to join a group who were going to the movies. Mom's worst fears were con-firmed when it turned out they were going to see *The Eddie Cantor Story.* Still, she didn't want to discourage Lloyd's first overture, so she agreed.

On Wednesday Mom was reminded by her hairdresser, Maxine, that she'd promised weeks before to entertain Maxine's son, Ronnie, who was in the air force, on his last night before he was shipped overseas. Ronnie, a big Eddie Cantor fan, wanted to catch *The Eddie Cantor Story* before leaving the States, and Mom didn't see how she could say no to a departing soldier.

On Saturday Mom did her marketing, and as on most Saturdays, Phil Hobaica, the apprentice butcher at Shadid's Market, gave her his best pitch for a date that very night. This time, however, she assented, even though Phil had suggested they spend the evening at the Plaza Theatre. Three nights prior, when Ronnie had taken her to the Plaza, she'd noted a banner announcing that *Forever Female* was to begin a weeklong run the very next night, and Mom had a huge crush on William Holden.

You can imagine her dismay when she learned that, in fact, *The Eddie Cantor Story* had been held over. She saw precious little of the film on this sixth viewing, however, as she spent most of the two hours fending off Phil's advances.

According to my father, Mom occasionally, even all these years later, recites lines from *The Eddie Cantor Story* in her sleep.

Bob Wills

MY parents hadn't been together very long when their friends
Don and Dorothy insisted they join them for an evening out, at
the Trianon Ballroom in downtown Oklahoma City. Bob Wills
and His Texas Playboys were the headliners, and their special
brand of Western swing kept the dance floor packed the whole
night long.

Wills managed to find Mom in the crowd, though, and he
clearly took a shine to her; from her first turn around the dance
floor, he couldn't take his eyes off of her. He tipped his huge
Stetson hat every time she turkey-trotted by and winked whenever he managed to catch her eye.

Wills was, by then, well into his fifties, and Mom, a young
woman at the peak of her beauty, certainly had no desire to en-
courage him. In fact, she did her utmost to avoid him altogether, but Don and my father, having a good time at Mom's
expense, kept swinging her right up stageside and turning her
so that she was forced to face the winking Wills.

Finally, the band took a break, and the two couples stepped out on the terrace for a breath of fresh air and a cigarette. When, after some time, they heard the orchestra strike up the opening strains of "Faded Love," Mom insisted they go back inside. This was her favorite Bob Wills tune, and she wanted to dance to it.

It wasn't long before Dad felt a tap-tap-tap upon his shoulder, signifying that someone was seeking to cut in, to take a turn around the floor with Mom. Surely by now you must have guessed that it was Wills. Dad graciously stepped aside, and Mom found herself firmly in Wills's clutches. She felt there was little she could do but make the best of the situation, grit her teeth and behave in gracious fashion until song's end. Already the vocalist had begun the second verse, and Mom held fast to the hope that this number would soon be over, allowing her to excuse herself and return to her table.

Just when the song would normally have wound down, however, Wills gave the high sign to the pianist, who signaled to the rest of the orchestra, and they took it again, right from the top. Now Mom felt, as Wills pulled her into a tighter embrace, his right hand slowly but steadily creeping downward, until it came to rest upon her left . . . well, let us say her left hip.

Mom fixed upon Wills an angry glare of an intensity that few have experienced and even fewer have survived. I have wilted under this glare not a few times myself, and believe me when I tell you, gentle reader, it's enough to make a strong man weep.

Wills was not up to the challenge. He quickly removed his hand, cleared his throat, tipped his hat, said, "Excuse me, ma'am," and hurriedly made his way back to the bandstand, whereupon he immediately called out for "Take Me Back to Tulsa" in double time.

Throughout the remainder of the evening, whenever Don or my father danced Mom within ten yards of the stage, Wills managed somehow to look busy, sorting through the musical charts on the bandstand, attending to an "out-of-tune" string on his fiddle, conducting the orchestra on a number they'd played hundreds of time.

During the second intermission, the waitress brought a round of beers to Mom and Dad's table and explained that they came compliments of the King of Western Swing himself, Bob Wills.

The Wager

I T all started one Saturday morning in September 1953. Mom and her good friends Patsy Standard, Barbara Gillespie, and Lola Hall made a habit of meeting for breakfast every Saturday morning at Beverly's on Lincoln Boulevard near Twenty-fourth Street. On this particular Saturday, Patsy made a big show of how tired she was after indulging in dates with two different men the night before. She'd gone to dinner and a movie with her near-steady, John Klingstedt, and then, having feigned a headache, met Dr. Greg Larkin, the new young orthodontist who'd just joined her dentist's practice, for a nightcap.

To the amusement of Barbara and Lola, Mom baited Patsy mercilessly, insisting that two dates was nothing at all, that she herself could easily manage three, four, even five dates in a day. Patsy asked if Mom might be willing to put her money where her mouth was. Sure, replied Mom, but what were to be the stakes in this wager?

Finally, it was agreed: If Mom could manage five dates in one day, Patsy would pay for her Saturday-morning breakfasts for the next six months. The rules were as follows: The first date was to begin no earlier than 6:00 A.M., and the last one must conclude by midnight. Her suitors were not to be told of the arrangement, and each date must last at least ninety minutes. They synchronized their watches, and the bet was on.

Mom was allotted only one week to amass these five requests for her company—it had been established that the dates had to take place the following Saturday—so she knew she'd have to work fast. She had an ace up her sleeve, though: Ron Wardlow, who'd been attending the Young Singles Sunday-school class at St. Luke's Methodist for the past few weeks, had been pestering Mom for a date for more than a month. Ron, a typesetter at Oklahoma Publishing Company, worked the overnight shift and didn't get off work until 5:30 A.M. So he was just the man to give Mom an early start on her campaign. She suggested that they meet for breakfast at seven—that would give him enough time to go home and give his ink-stained hands a good scrubbing—and he immediately agreed.

Gavin Garrett, son of the founder and president of the company for which Mom worked as a secretary, Garrett Grommett Corp., was fresh out of college and working his way up the ladder at his father's business. His ascent would be a rapid one, but his father insisted that Gavin work for at least three months in every department in the company so that he might learn the business from the ground up. Just then Gavin was working in Accounts Receivable, where Mom worked, and he had, on more than one occasion, expressed an interest in seeing Mom somewhere other than the office.

Gavin had been a tennis player in college, and Mom knew he'd leap at the chance to impress her with his fore- and backhands, not to mention his serve. So she suggested a late-morning tennis date at, say, eleven o'clock? Gavin happily agreed, and Mom was two fifths of the way home.

Mom has always been an avid reader, but in those days her budget was quite limited. So every Sunday afternoon she stopped by her local branch library to return the books she'd read that week and select a new title or two.

Larry Knutson was the Sunday librarian at the branch nearest Mom's apartment. Painfully shy and more than a little awkward, with a cowlicky mane of hair that simply refused to be tamed by even the most dominating of hair oils, Larry was hardly Mom's idea of the ideal man, but he was sweet and good-natured, and among the men of Mom's acquaintance, he was the only one who shared her love of classical music. So it was that Mom and Larry, unbeknownst to anyone, had gone in together to purchase a pair of season passes to a special series of Saturday-afternoon concerts put on by the Oklahoma City symphony. So the third slot in Mom's lineup on that Saturday would be filled by her standing date with Larry.

Mom's fourth date was almost as easy to arrange. She'd made a habit, the last three or four weeks, of spending her Saturday nights with Lloyd Leveridge. He played catcher for the St. Luke's fast-pitch softball team, and she and a couple of the other gals from church had been attending the games every Saturday evening. Lloyd was always pleased to have her in the stands, although her presence did precipitate just the slightest bit of nervousness on his part. His batting average had suffered as a result, falling by some twenty points in the few short weeks she'd been attending the games.

Now Mom had only to arrange a late-night rendezvous and her victory would be assured. She decided to visit Patsy's dentist for a cleaning, in hopes that she'd have the chance to meet and impress his new young partner, Dr. Larkin, the very man who'd kept Patsy out late the week before.

Dr. Larkin spotted Mom in the waiting room and wandered over to introduce himself. He was a go-getter, was Dr. Larkin, and well before Mom was summoned by the dental assistant to come in for her cleaning, he had secured both her phone number and a promise to join him for a nightcap at ten on Saturday night.

And so the stage was set; all five dates were arranged. Mom knew she needed only take care to stick to her schedule to achieve the satisfaction of winning the bet and the luxury of six months of free Saturday breakfasts.

Things began smoothly. Ron appeared at Mom's door at the appointed hour, and she was pleased to see that he'd rid his hands of most of the ink stains left by his night's work. Breakfast was pleasant enough, and when the waiter brought the check at 8:31, it was clear Mom had successfully managed the first date of the day.

But it was not that simple. Ron had been waiting a long time for this date, and though he'd worked all night, he was not at all tired. Nine in the morning was for him like nine in the evening for someone who kept more regular hours. He wouldn't be ready to hit the hay for two or three more hours, and he was intent upon spending those hours with Mom. To her credit, Mom didn't panic; after all, Gavin wasn't due until ten-thirty. She and Ron sat and chatted, gently swaying in the porch swing that hung just beside the front door to the small apartment house where she lived. Mom kept a close but surreptitious eye on her watch, and when ten o'clock rolled around, she explained to Ron that she really must go. She'd been up all night with a toothache, she fibbed, and the lack of sleep was now catching up with her.

With Ron dispatched, Mom scurried upstairs and changed into her tennis togs. No sooner had she tied the laces on her bright white tennis shoes than Gavin arrived for her in his brand-new MG convertible. Mom tossed her racket in behind her seat, and they were off to the Nichols Hills Country Club, where the Garretts were charter members.

Mom was a fairly accomplished tennis player herself—she'd lettered in her sophomore year of high school—but Gavin was top-notch. He was gentleman enough to allow Mom to win her share of games, but when the two teamed up to take on another couple in doubles, he let go with his A game. They swept that three-set match 6–1, 6–2, 6–love, and it was only after Gavin's ace at match point that Mom thought to check her watch. She panicked a bit when she realized that she'd let time get away from her, that it was now half past noon. Larry was to pick her up at one-thirty for the concert, and she and Gavin faced at least a twenty-minute drive through Saturday traffic to reach her apartment.

To make matters worse, as they reached Gavin's MG, he opened the trunk to reveal a rather fancy picnic lunch, complete with a chilled bottle of white wine. Mom was famished after the tennis and the food looked delicious, but she clearly had no time for indulging Gavin, who seemed crushed when Mom insisted he take her right home. To assuage his hurt feelings, she feigned a sinus headache—the pollen had been especially heavy that spring—and promised Gavin a raincheck on the picnic lunch.

Mom had just barely finished sprucing up for the concert when her landlady announced that Larry had arrived. They walked, as they usually did, the dozen or so blocks to the Civic Center, Mom worrying that the concert might prove to be a lengthy one. Lloyd's softball game was scheduled for six o'clock, and they had agreed that he would pick her up at five-thirty. Still, most of these Saturday concerts lasted only a couple of hours, which would allow Mom ample time to get home and change into something suitable for the ballpark.

She and Larry made it to their seats just as the musicians were giving their instruments a final tuning, and the concert commenced promptly at two. Mom was pleased to learn that the first piece was a short one—Barber's Adagio for Strings in G, one of her favorites. Next up was Brahms's First Symphony, a tidy forty-five minutes long. The ten-minute intermission was to be followed by a Mahler symphony, and though it was a piece unfamiliar to Mom, she assumed she'd be on her way home no later than four-fifteen. Perhaps she would even manage to squeeze in a catnap before Lloyd arrived. A reasonable hope, except the Mahler symphony was his Second, which clocks in at just under two hours. It was 5:05 before the final notes were sounded. Worst of all, as they reached the front door of her building, shy, awkward Larry made his first, bumbling attempt at a pass at Mom. Larry—who had yet to screw up the courage necessary even to ask Mom for her phone number, who had never attempted even to kiss her on the cheek or hold her hand, who had never so much as slipped his arm around Mom's waist as they walked to the Civic Center on those Saturday afternoons—now, perhaps transformed by the passion and majesty of Mahler's Second, had Mom firmly in his trembling but insistent clutches. Mom knew she could handle Larry, who was clearly in over his head, but she feared that if she didn't act quickly, Lloyd, of whom she was growing rather fond, might pull up at any moment and find her in Larry's arms.

Thinking that a pedestrian excuse like a headache or common weariness might not quickly enough dissuade the newly impassioned Larry, Mom revealed, with feigned embarrassment, that she was experiencing "monthly discomfort," that she really felt that she should go lie down with a hot-water bottle.

That was, of course, just the slap in the face that Larry needed; apologizing profusely, he made his red-faced exit posthaste—and without a moment to spare, for no sooner had Mom reached her upstairs apartment than her landlady informed her that Lloyd was calling for her. Mom hurriedly changed clothes and joined him.

As they drove toward Wheeler Park and its complex of softball fields, Mom assessed her status. She'd so far successfully managed three of the five required dates and still had nearly seven hours to squeeze in the last two. She sighed contentedly, convinced that victory would be hers and without too much further difficulty.

Fast-pitch softball is an unpredictable game, however, and when Mom and Lloyd arrived at Field 3, they found the preceding game still in progress. The two teams had battled through softball's seven regulation innings tied at 1 and were now entering extra innings. Mom had not accounted for this; Lloyd's game could not begin until this one came to an end, of course, and it appeared that both pitchers were on top of their games. The eighth inning saw no scoring; nor did the ninth and tenth. In the top of the eleventh, a grapefruit of a change-up was sent over the left-field wall, but it drifted just foul.

Finally, in the bottom of the eleventh, two singles and a hit batsman loaded the bases, and the pitcher, now a bit rattled, walked in the winning run on four pitches.

Still, Lloyd and the rest of the St. Luke's ten didn't take the field until nearly seven. Their game went only the regulation seven innings, but it was a slow-moving contest. Lloyd had a great night behind the plate: In the first five innings, he threw out three different runners attempting to steal second; in the sixth inning he blocked the plate and made the tag on a very close play at home, and in the bottom of the seventh he overcame the nerves Mom's presence in the stands usually inspired to drive in the tying and winning runs with a bases-loaded double. Though he was the modest sort, Lloyd was clearly so proud of his night's accomplishments that Mom couldn't bring herself to spoil his big night by conjuring another excuse and asking him to take her home early. But the game had lasted until nearly nine o'clock, and Dr. Larkin was due to call for Mom at ten.

As they usually did, the players and their wives and dates went to a Carnation ice cream parlor for a postgame treat. It was a short ten-block walk from her apartment, so no sooner had the sundaes been served than Mom made it a point to spill a banana split with extra hot fudge all over herself. She refused Lloyd's offer of a lift home, insisting instead upon walking home alone. That way Lloyd could stay behind and continue to revel in the afterglow of his game-winning heroics. She'd shower and change, she assured him, and come right back.

Of course she had no intention of returning. Once home, she called Lloyd at the ice cream parlor and told him that the warm shower had made her sleepy and would he understand if she just stayed home? Of course he understood, he assured her, thereby freeing her to concentrate on the final date of the day.

But ten o'clock rolled around and there was no sign of Dr. Larkin. What to do? The date had to commence by ten-thirty, or the bet was lost. Finally, at 10:18, he called. He'd gotten a flat tire about a mile from Mom's place and had only now managed to change it and make his way to a pay phone.

Dr. Larkin had it in mind to take Mom to the Silver Lounge, a tony nightspot in the Hotel Black, but Mom, trying to salvage the bet, insisted on meeting him instead at the Cock o' the Walk, a beer joint that was just a few blocks from her apartment. He protested, but she insisted she'd meet him there in five minutes and hung up the phone. Mom slipped on a pair of flats and ran all the way to the Cock o' the Walk. She arrived, perspiring and out of breath, at 10:27 and took a seat at the end of the bar, a spot that gave her a clear view of the establishment's entrance. Mom was sweating bullets as her eyes shifted from her watch to the bar's front door and back again. Finally, at 10:29 and 18 seconds, Dr. Larkin walked in the door, looking more than a little out of place in his hand-tailored suit and silk tie.

Mom was certain she was home free, but after a few minutes over a cold glass of beer, Dr. Larkin admitted that he was feeling more than a bit intimidated by the truck drivers, delivery men, and other laborers who comprised the Cock o' the Walk's clientele. Mom feared he'd panic and find an excuse to cut the date short before the required ninety minutes had passed, so she took the bull by the horns. When he wasn't looking, she undid a button on her cotton blouse, touched him lightly on the arm, and, whispering breathlessly in his ear, suggested that they retire to a booth in the back. Now putty in her hands, he readily agreed. She spent the remainder of the date fending off his amorous advances—not an entirely pleasant way to spend eighty minutes but nothing she couldn't handle—and when her watch read 11:55, she offered her showiest yawn and insisted Dr. Larkin drive her home immediately. He never knew what hit him.

Home and in her pajamas by 12:15 A.M., Mom called Patsy, knowing full well she'd be asleep, and informed her that the five dates had, in fact, been successfully negotiated. Patsy could only laugh. The following Saturday found Mom, Patsy, Barbara, and Lola once again at Beverly's Café, only this time—and every Saturday for the ensuing six months—Mom's hearty breakfast of bacon, eggs, hash browns, and toast with jam was on Patsy.

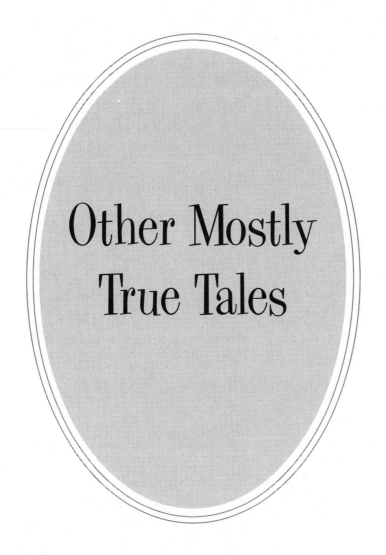

Other Mostly
True Tales

My Life Among the Elite

I T ' S not always easy to recognize life's turning points, but occasionally they make themselves perfectly clear.

It's late afternoon, and I'm standing on a midtown Manhattan subway platform, waiting for the downtown #1 train. The platform is moderately crowded, but fifty or sixty feet away, a figure catches my eye.

He's a young man, no more than thirty-two or thirty-three. Five foot ten or so, dark hair, pasty complexion, a little pudgy. He's making his way slowly along the platform, speaking briefly to every person there. He makes eye contact with each individual as he nears, a certain demented fervor reflected in his gaze.

One might assume he's making a pitch for spare change, but as he draws near enough to be audible, one learns it is not a plea he offers but an assessment, a judgment, an approval or a dismissal of each and every person he encounters.

"*You*—you're out!" he proclaims to one stranger who is found lacking.

"*You*—gone!" Another one bites the dust.

"*You*—you can stay."

"*You*—outta here."

And so it goes. No justification is offered for his pronouncements. Whatever his guidelines, he chooses not to share them. He doesn't strike one as threatening, and he makes no attempt to act on his verdicts. The announcing of them is what he is about. One is in or one is out, that's it, case closed.

Easy, you might think, to dismiss him as just another subway eccentric, but the effect he has on those he addresses is undeniable. At first, each feigns disinterest, but eventually, as the moment of truth draws nigh, as their assessor approaches, one can sense the anxiety, the panic even, as each person—man, woman, and child—awaits his or her judgment.

I, too, am but a man, only flesh and blood, and try as I might to remain unconcerned with his progress along the platform, I find myself casting the occasional askance glance his way. Now only five or six people separate me from my moment of the truth, and I can feel my heart pounding within my chest. My mouth going cotton-dry, and the slightest tic—just a little twitch—appears over my right eye.

Meanwhile, the fiftyish woman in the business suit and thick glasses is summarily dismissed.

The homie in the baggy shorts and Chicago Bulls jersey makes the cut.

The young immigrant mother, who seems not to grasp the import of this moment, is given the okay.

The bookish man in the maroon cardigan sweater, with balding head and red face, is cut loose with particular relish.

The young woman with the tattoos and the piercings and the Astor Place haircut is looked upon favorably.

And now it is my turn. All noise ceases. I become immune to all other external stimuli. It is as if there is no one else in the world but this man, this gatekeeper, this sentry, this dean of underground admissions, and me. And it is with an exalted sense of relief that I hear him pronounce, in authoritarian tones . . .

"*You* can stay."

O, sweet acceptance! To be among the selected, the honored, the chosen few.

I find myself, against my own better judgment, now looking with some disdain and perhaps a tinge of pity upon those who didn't make the cut. How terrible to be excluded, to be found unworthy! But no one has ever claimed life to be fair, have they? I choose not to dwell on why some are chosen and others cast aside. I prefer to revel in my newfound status, my new life among the elite.

A Rosebud by
Any Other Name

THERE seems to be a steady market for those books that offer hundreds of names for expectant parents to consider for their new baby, but I sometimes wonder why. Let's face it, most people take the safe route, opting for the pedestrian in dubbing their new arrival, be it Tom, Dick, or Harriet. Who needs a book to come up with Bob?

If I were anxiously awaiting a blessed event, I believe I'd prefer a guide to those rather more sticky decisions that a young couple must confront, i.e., what little nicknames are to be used for the child's genitals and bodily functions? This is so daunting a quandary as to keep me up nights.

I would certainly want to do all I could to ensure that my child grew up without excessive inhibitions and with a healthy attitude regarding his or her body and sexuality. And it seems to me that a key to this effort would be the selection of pseudonyms of a personal nature that I could say without giggling. I certainly wouldn't wish to pass on to my son, for example, the notion that there was anything laughable about his . . . um, *willy.* Nor would I wish to give my daughter the impression that . . . er, *piddling* is anything to be embarrassed about.

And I'd be terribly dismayed to learn, years from now, that Brett Jr. was devoting his valuable time and hard-earned money to therapy in an attempt to deal with the fact that his father had forced him to call his penis "Mr. Happy" or "Little Brett" or "Oscar Mayer" or . . . well, you get the idea.

I really cringe, though, when I imagine the spousal discussion of this matter. What a horrid reason for a fight: "Okay, tell me. Explain to me, please, what is so wrong with *doody*?" "I don't know, I'm just not comfortable with it." "Well, *doody* was good enough for my parents, and I don't understand why it's not good enough for us!"

I suspect that the primary reason we opt for these biological aliases is the potential for public embarrassment. I, for one, am not so mature—so evolved, if you will—as to feel comfortable having my child exclaim in the produce section of the A&P, "Daddy, I have to urinate!" On the other hand, I don't believe anyone is fooled by the terms *tinkle, wee-wee,* or *pee-pee,* either. So I think I may attempt to advance the process a step further. Why not come up with a code that is a little tougher to crack than, say, *number one* and *number two*? What if, when your child felt nature's call in that same A&P, he proclaimed, "Man, could I go for some couscous right about now!" or "We must re-member, Daddy, to tape *Diagnosis: Murder* tonight!" or even "How about those Mets?" With a little planning, you'd know just what your child was trying to tell you, and Sal the stockboy would be none the wiser.

Gay Like Me

I was in Tower Records recently looking for the Fifth Dimension's *Greatest Hits* as a birthday present for my mother. They had moved the oldies section since my previous visit, and a nearby clerk, perhaps noticing that I seemed disoriented, approached me and said, "Show tunes are upstairs."

He could hardly have provided less appropriate information. I don't like show tunes, and I wondered why he had assumed that I do.

"He thought you were gay," a friend offered when I related my experience, "and so assumed that you must like show tunes." I'll admit that this explanation had occurred to me too, but it raised another question: Even if I were gay, why did the clerk assume that I would like show tunes?

It wasn't the first time a stranger had decided I was gay. When I was in college, I was walking to class on a warm spring afternoon when a young woman I'd never seen before turned to me as we passed each other and spat out, "Faggot!" It caught me so off guard, I was certain I'd misunderstood her. "Was she talking to me?" I asked my classmate. "And what did she say?" "She called you a faggot," he answered, as baffled as I was. I didn't know then and don't know now what made her so certain that I was gay, but I was even more puzzled that she'd decided to lash out, to confront me in such an abusive fashion.

That was my initiation into the queer life. And many years later, I'm no less of a magnet for strangers' anti-gay venom. While I've lived in New York City, on any number of occasions I've found myself embroiled in a disagreement. I stand up for myself after being cut off in a crosswalk by an impatient cabbie, or shoved in a crowded subway by someone determined to impinge upon my already limited personal space—only to have the aggressor let loose with the same hateful epithet I heard on the way to class all those years ago.

The fact that I'm not gay hardly matters in these instances. Something about my hair, my voice, my walk—who knows?—puts these people off, and they don't hesitate to let me know it. It's easier to hate someone after you've got him neatly packaged and labeled, so the cabbie who slathers me with the homosexual brush likely doesn't care that his assumption is incorrect. To him, someone who looks, talks, or walks the way I do must be a fag, and that's just fine with me.

After all, there are many positive aspects to gay stereotypes; perhaps by assuming that I'm gay, that cabbie is also guessing that I'm fastidious in my personal hygiene, that I'm nimble on the dance floor, that I keep a tidy apartment. Since I am possessed of only one of those attributes—although I do shower at least once a day, I'm not much of a dancer and my apartment usually has a ransacked look that suggests a recent burglary—if strangers want to assign to me such admirable qualities, then what the heck.

Still, I'm not sure why it is—in a time when even relatively un-enlightened people have learned to at least hold their tongues—that gay men are still considered fair game for such verbal and even physical assaults. Maybe it's the stereotype that gay men are all sissies—that when push comes to shove, any straight man could handle a gay man in a fight.

That's patently ridiculous, of course. Though I am heterosexual, I'm also a fairly committed pacifist and a resolute and un-wavering coward, and therefore completely unschooled in the art of fisticuffs. I have no doubt that most men—straight, gay, or undecided—could use me to mop up the sidewalk if they so chose. That's really the only problem I have now with my status as an honorary gay man: the fear that one of these nights I'll be subject to a little honorary gay-bashing. But I suppose that if my reputation as a dancer and housekeeper is to benefit from my being presumed gay, it's only right and fair that I assume the same risks gay men and lesbians have so long endured.

Walk Like a Man

O N E thing that really sets my teeth on edge is gender-based stereotyping. You know the routine: Men fear commitment, hate to shop, withhold emotions, and love tools. Women, on the other hand, hate sports, can't drive, and are bad tippers.

Can it be that I am not truly male but instead the *anti-male*, possessed of all the surface elements required of that gender but not the inner makeup, lacking a certain something . . . a gene, a chromosome? Perhaps my testosterone tank requires a fill-up. Lord knows, if I listened to the experts, from Tim Allen to whoever creates those quizzes in *Cosmopolitan* magazine, I'd be one perplexed fellow.

Think you, perhaps, that I exaggerate? Consider, then, this litany of red herrings: I have, more than once, refused sex. I can spend hours on end browsing in stores, provided, that is, that I'm to be the recipient of the impending bounty. I can't tell a crescent wrench from a crescent roll. I hug other men freely—I even kiss my father. I've never set foot in a strip club. I couldn't care less what's under the hood of a car, as long as the sum of those various and sundry parts is purring like a kitten. I like foreign films. I can't build anything. I can't fix anything and don't particularly have the desire to. I stop and ask directions at the first hint that I might have lost my way.

Present the above profile to, say, Dr. Joyce Brothers, and I'm willing to bet she'd peg me as female.

And yet, even I must admit, certain gender-based tendencies simply can't be denied. For instance, while I have known only a handful of men over the years who enjoy dancing, I don't believe I've ever met a woman who didn't. Many, in fact, place the ability to dance very high on the shopping list of traits they seek in a partner. Now, I am not terribly fond of dancing myself. And yet, I think I could manage the occasional session of rug cutting if I didn't know full well just how much importance many, if not most, women place on this activity. One can almost see the mental checking-off as it occurs: "Let's see . . . looks? Passable. Gainfully employed? Yes. Good sense of humor? Check. Intelligent? Yep. And how would you characterize his dancing? I'd have to say it most closely resembles a spastic seal playing Charades." And that's it. Game's over. Hit the showers.

Better, then, I suspect, to opt for the crusty, contrarian, stick-in-the-mud approach. She'll more easily forgive that than a set of two left feet and no sense of rhythm.

Perhaps the biggest difference between the sexes, however, lies in the willingness, or lack thereof, to share clothes. Women seem to have no qualms whatsoever about this practice. In fact, I have known women who chose their roommates almost exclusively based on their wardrobe. I, on the other hand, have never borrowed another man's garments, and if I live to be a hundred, I don't believe I ever will. There's something . . . I don't know, *creepy* about wearing someone else's clothes. My clothes, for better or worse, say something about who I am (mostly, they say, "Here is a man who washes whites and colors together in warm water and never uses bleach"). To wear someone else's clothes strikes me as a sort of sartorial lie. I would feel no less sullied than if I were to lie to an evening's companion about my age or my occupation. I mean, why stop at clothes? Why not borrow a friend's car, if it would impress the young woman? Why not appropriate a friend's interests, his likes and dislikes, his pet peeves, his rich and varied past? His dreams and aspirations?

I actually take a certain comfort from the fact that these two vital, undeniable differences between the sexes exist. My aversion to dancing and my refusal to swap shirts with a buddy place me squarely in the "real men" camp, in spite of my many other failings. And I sleep better at night as a result.

Motorless in Manhattan

Not so long ago I gave my nephew, Matthew, a subscription to *Mad* magazine. I was a subscriber when I was his age, and it seemed an appropriate gift. This backfired on me, however, during a recent visit home. Matt showed me an article from a recent issue, one that contained a pie chart illustrating a breakdown of the various ways in which people end up subscribing to that publication. One small slice of that pie, representing 11 percent of the total, was labeled "Gift subscriptions from that weird uncle who never married."

Matt and I had a good laugh over my being so thoroughly and completely pegged, but the more I think about it, the more I wonder: *Am I weird?* There's no denying that I'm single, but does that, in and of itself, make me weird? It depends, I suspect, upon the set of accepted standards by which one is judging. Perhaps in Oklahoma City I could safely be judged at least a little odd, but not necessarily so in the Big Apple. The fact that I have, at my age, never been married sets me distinctly apart from the norm in Oklahoma. But then, so does the fact that I've never owned a car. In fact, the combination of these two characteristics may classify me as utterly unique in the Sooner State. It's difficult to imagine a person of my years residing there who has not managed one or the other of these feats. But in New York City I am a member of a large, if to date unorganized, fellowship of single people who have no wheels. In fact, many people here have never even learned to drive, much less possessed the title on a motor vehicle.

The question I ask myself, therefore, is not how it is that I have failed to find, by now, an appropriate mate, but rather, how is it so many others have managed to pair up so easily? The odds against success in this field of endeavor seem terribly long to me, truth be told.

If you will, gentle reader, allow me to pursue a bit further the analogy between car ownership and marriage, I believe I can illustrate my point.

If I were to awaken tomorrow possessed by the desire to own a car, I'm not sure I'd even know where to begin, any more than I know where to turn to find Ms. Right. After all, there are literally dozens of makes and hundreds of models from which to choose. I suppose I could attend a new-car show, wander from showroom to showroom, perhaps even hire a broker. But these approaches edge too near the tactics of desperate lonely hearts; they are the automotive equivalents of pickup bars, singles events, and computer-dating services. And while it's true that the car of one's dreams is not going to pull up in front of one's house and honk, desperation is unattractive, whether one is seeking companionship or transportation. Perhaps best, then, to go about one's business and not focus too intently on the search. Oh, sure, one should keep one's eyes open; one never knows when just the right car will pull up at the intersection. But to seek out one's dream vehicle, to actively search for it, is, I fear, to invite disappointment.

It is important, too, to consider the level of involvement to which one is willing to commit. Perhaps you're not really ready to buy. It may be that the occasional rental will fulfill your needs, or perhaps even a short-term lease.

One must also be careful not to sacrifice reliability to the pursuit of surface beauty. After all, a nice chassis and beautiful paint job might be eye-catching, but they won't last forever. Time will bring its dents, pings, and scratches. Far more important that your pride and joy start easily on cold mornings, that it not break down and leave you stranded, that it not be so eye-catching as to attract the attention of those who might not be above stealing it in the night. For it's not necessarily better to have driven and lost than never to have driven at all.

Suffer in Silence

I often bemoan the fact that advertising is, at its core, false and misleading. The truth is dispensed with posthaste, if not ignored altogether, and those men in gray flannel get on about the business of filling our heads with nonsensical promises of things never to be.

Buy a particular brand of beer and turn a nothing day into a glorious adventure. Find yourself magically transported into another dimension where time and space are malleable, where the blazing summer sun instantly gives way to a bracing winter's day. Almost inexplicably, you now possess mystical powers heretofore unimagined. And beautiful, saucy, sassy women who previously would not have given you the time of day now find you suddenly irresistible. All this, for the price of a lager.

Or, if you're willing to spend a bit more, commit to that special make of automobile and you'll find that your whole life has done a 180. You're smart, attractive. The babes won't leave you alone. Those suits you bought on sale at K mart are suddenly well tailored and of the finest fabrics. You enjoy a new sense of respect from your peers, and suddenly you're on the fast track, careerwise. All this and rack-and-pinion steering, too.

It's utter nonsense, of course—reprehensively obvious hucksterism—and I find myself gnashing my teeth as I endure these thirty-second snow jobs. But if the alternative is the reality revealed to us by the likes of Gold Bond Medicated Powder, then, brother, tell me lies, tell me sweet little lies. These repellent confessionals, filled as they are by people with bad grammar, worse hair, and itching skin conditions, are just about more than I can take.

How do the Gold Bond people excavate these prickly unfortunates? What's their methodology? Perhaps they have informants in sheriff's offices around the country who fill them in when there's a trailer-park eviction pending. Or maybe they paid good money for the *Weekly World News* mailing list. It could even be they just drive about, looking for lawns studded with plaster gnomes, plastic deer, and vintage Dodge Darts hoisted on blocks.

It's not that I can't feel sympathy for their suffering, but in the name of all that's decent, can't they try to bear their dry, flaky crosses with some dignity? I believe it's true that we never walk alone, but if you're chafing, please, keep it to yourself.

Strangest of all is how familiar some of these faces look. I'm convinced that the Gold Bond company and Publishers Clearing House are in cahoots, that one season's heat-rash victim is the next season's lucky winner. I mean, how else could they prod these miserables into spilling the details of their itchy, flaky hell on national television, except by dangling a new fishing boat or prefab vacation home in front of them?

The Curse of Cupid

As a single man I find myself viewing the buildup to Valentine's Day much as I imagine American Jews, Muslims, and Buddhists might perceive the hustle and bustle of the Christmas season: much ado but nothing to do with me.

It doesn't help that this is one holiday not merely co-opted by commercial interests but seemingly created by them. Don't get me wrong, I'm no Scrooge when it comes to matters of the heart. Quite the contrary, I'm a sucker for anything romantic. The product of a loving marriage of forty-five years, I was raised to believe in happily ever after.

In past years I've gamely opted for alternate ways of observing the holiday: gifts to my mother, dime-store valentines for my female coworkers, bowls of those little candy hearts for all to share. But it's a shallow charade. If you can't celebrate Valentine's Day with passion, you really can't celebrate it at all. I feel like the out-of-work actor who has to watch some Hollywood pretty boy get not only the part but the money, the fame, *and* the Oscar. I can no longer pretend to be all that happy for all you lovebirds.

For single people everywhere who lack the affection, devotion, companionship, and support—not to mention the physical pleasures—that a romantic relationship offers, Valentine's Day serves as a rude reminder that they are on the outside looking in.

Look at it this way: Imagine that we had a national holiday that celebrated the state of having a job. All who were gainfully employed would spend the day musing on their good fortune: how much better their lives are with a steady income, how nice it is to have the security, to know where their next meal is coming from. Perhaps we'd even surprise our employers with a bouquet of flowers, a box of candy, or a night on the town. It doesn't sound so bad, I suppose, but it'd be a little rough on the unemployed. Just one more reminder of what they're missing. Such is Valentine's Day for the unattached.

So maybe, just maybe, February 14 should be devoted instead to us third wheels. I'm reasonably certain that we've not yet been assigned a patron saint, so perhaps we should just co-opt yours. Here's what I'm envisioning for an alternative Valentine's Day celebration: Every couple invites over a friend who's unattached, and just for one night, they live out their worst fantasy of what couplehood might be like. She comes to the door with her hair in rollers and cold cream on her face; he's unshaven and wearing a ratty undershirt. The fare is frozen pizza and warm beer served on trays in front of a blaring television. The hosts spend the entire evening pointing out each other's many deficiencies until he finally falls asleep on the couch and she wanders off to bed alone. That'd be enough to make most lovesick lonely hearts swear they weren't missing a thing, that perhaps the single life wasn't so bad after all.

So c'mon, couples across America, it's the least you can do. For just one night, convince the rest of us that love stinks.

A Little Magic in the Night

THREE A.M. on a Sunday night when sleep is elusive. I've gotten to bed a bit later than usual and have tossed and turned for an hour or more. But finally, finally I manage to drift into the early stages of slumber, only to have a rapid scuffing sound, outside the window next to my bed, begin to peck its way into my consciousness. In my dreamy state, I imagine that someone is rhythmically scraping at bricks, that perhaps my super is making some inexplicably ill-timed repairs to the outer wall of my building.

But why, I ask myself in my still-submerged state, would Alex do such work at this ungodly hour? What masonry emergency could be so dire as to require patching in the wee hours? But wait—as I continue to ascend toward wakefulness, the sound now strikes me as more closely resembling the bouncing of a basketball on the sidewalk outside my second-floor apartment—but by an especially adept dribbler. So why, I wonder, would the Harlem Globetrotters be running drills outside my building in the middle of the night? Don't they have a gym somewhere they could use?

As I grow more alert, I realize, of course, that it's likely not the Globetrotters but rather some neighborhood kids, who ought to be home in bed, working on their ball-handling skills. I roll over, wrapping my pillow around my head in an attempt to muffle the noise of their dribbling, but it's no use.

As the minutes tick by, the noise sounds less and less like a basketball on concrete. These are rhythms that would do Tito Puente proud; if it's the sound of dribbling I'm hearing, it's the work of one helluva ball handler. Throwing in the towel on a quick return to slumber and now quite agitated, I sit up and kneel on my bed so that I can look out the window.

My anger quickly subsides as I view, on this crystal-clear night, in the warm glow of a nearly full moon, four men who stand facing one another in a tight circle beneath my window. They are tap dancers—soft-shoe dancers, really—trading eights, each in turn strutting his stuff, creating enchantingly syncopated rhythms with only his feet.

As I watch, the youngest of the group, a man of perhaps twenty-two years, is taking his turn. He wears baggy jeans and a white T-shirt, and his intent expression stands in stark contrast to the easy joy of the other men, each of whom is his elder, and by some years. They, it seems, have learned to relax and let it go, to trust that their feet will not fail them. But the young man earnestly endeavors to perform steps he may well have spent the entire day conjuring. It may be that his teacher is among this group; perhaps they are all his teachers. But he is clearly relieved when his turn, his eight bars, have passed. It shows in the sudden, relaxed droop of his shoulders and in the gentle arc of his fingers as his hands hang at his sides.

As he stops, the man to his right picks up the rhythm. He is a portly fellow in his fifties, and though his moves are subtler, less flashy than the young man's, his sheer delight in the internal rhythms that are guiding his feet is obvious. The moonlight reflects off his shiny, coffee-colored pate, and as he reaches the end of his routine, he throws back his head, laughing, exulting in the moment.

He turns and, like a relay racer passing off a baton, slaps five with the third dancer, who stands well over six feet tall and is rail thin. He wears a sly, knowing grin as he shuffles his feet, stepping back just a bit from the circle so that he can raise his long, thin arms—first his right and then his left—straight out to his sides as if to balance himself. He is a bit showier than were the dancers preceding him; he bends forward at the waist, swings his outstretched arms to and fro, and finally removes the baseball cap from his head, bowing deep to an audience only he can hear.

Now the eldest of the group, a man who must be at least sixty-five and, judging by his shock of white hair, may be as old as eighty, is already dancing. His steps are almost imperceptible—I can't even hear the shuffling of his shoes against the pavement—but he clearly lives for moments like this, relishing the opportunity to surrender, even in his limited fashion, to those same rhythms that the three younger men had marked with their feet, to perpetuate, in the pale glow of a late-spring moon, what surely must now be, for him, several decades of dancing. His are slow and steady movements, long, scraping sweeps of the foot, like a drummer using brushes instead of sticks, but they seem wonderfully economical after the feverish steps of the younger men.

I watch, captivated, for two or three laps around this circle of dancers. There is nowhere I'd rather be at this moment, and the thought of rolling over and trying to will myself to sleep is now singularly unappealing. I find myself cursing my nine-to-five job and longing for my bartending days, when my schedule was my own and if I wanted to stay up all night, I did. I toy with the notion of arriving late at the office and blaming it on a broken alarm clock or even calling in sick, but it's a busy time of the year and I have a stack of work awaiting me. So it is with a deep sigh of regret that I reach up and rap three or four times on the windowpane. The four men pause as one and look up. Their gentle faces show just a hint of surprised alarm, and one of them says, "Sorry! Sorry, buddy. Don't call the cops on us."

I give them a wave of reassurance, and they gather their bags and jackets before moving on. I watch as they wander down the street to the east. After they drift out of sight, I lie back in my bed and marvel at the gifts a night in the city can yield.

The Agony of Defeat

I T is the waning moments of CBS's coverage of the championship game of the 1994 College World Series. The favored Georgia Tech Yellow Jackets are just an out or two away from falling to the Oklahoma Sooners, 13–5. Soon enough, Brent Musburger will be waxing poetic about the victorious Sooners, but now it is time to throw a commentator's bone to the vanquished nine.

You know the routine: "courageous effort . . . talented young athletes . . . no real losers in a game like this . . . they should hold their heads high." It's trite stuff but, no doubt, well intended. As this by-rote recitation unfolds, we, the viewers, are treated to a slow pan down the length of the Georgia Tech bench. One after the other, the dejected faces of the Yellow Jackets, struggling to come to terms with their defeat, appears on-screen. This young man's face reveals sadness, that one defiance. Disappointment is reflected in this lad's countenance, while stoic resolve is found in the set jaw of another.

But now the camera pauses on the face of an unnamed Yellow Jacket. He neither weeps nor curses. His face is creased by neither smile nor frown. He seems, in fact, almost detached—distracted, somehow—as he digs his finger deeper and deeper into his left nostril, in search of what we can only guess.

Such is the nature of live TV coverage, of course. Sports fans are accustomed to the occasional spit shot of a tobacco-chewing combatant, the odd on-field genital rearrangement, a lip-read profanity from time to time. These things happen, and every now and then the camera will capture the action. Usually, though, an astute director calls for a quick switch to another camera, a new view, that saves the offending gladiator further embarrassment and preserves the home viewers' sensibilities.

Not this day. Millions across the country watch as that young man picks his nose and the camera lingers. Five seconds pass, six, seven seconds—not long in the life of a man but an eternity on television—and still the young man keeps his digit deeply imbedded in his nasal passage, digging, ever digging. Eight seconds, nine seconds . . .

When finally the young man removes his finger and takes a good long look at what he's extracted, the director loses his nerve. Even he, it seems, has his limits. After all, for all he knows, this nasal prospector might next decide to ingest his bounty, and who among us could take that scene? Instead, thankfully, the Sooners at last make the final putout and the camera again focuses on the field to capture the celebration.

I've thought of that young man since, though. How humiliated he must feel! I'm certain that everyone he knows was watching that day, and I'm sure that not a few of them have informed him, in deriding fashion, that they hung in until the final out, that they didn't miss his moment of glory. Perhaps his time in the spotlight received coverage in the *Atlanta Journal-Constitution*. There's little doubt his moment in the sun was discussed on the local sports talk-radio shows. He even made the pages of this book. The agony of defeat, indeed!

Crying Uncle on Fatherhood

As a fortyish man who has not, to date, brought forth any progeny, I find myself feeling just a bit envious when Father's Day rolls around. Any celebration that elicits presents, a favorite meal, and praise and gratitude from those who care for me is one I'm ready to sign on for. Father's Day boasts all the benefits of a birthday without the unpleasant aging issues.

Of course, to earn a birthday celebration, all one must really do is a) be born and b) manage somehow to stick around. Fathers must hoe a much tougher row before being awarded their annual supply of ties, golf paraphernalia, and war books. And therein, for me, lies the rub.

If ever I were to become a dad, I hope that I would prove to be a devoted one, but I'm afraid there are certain paternal duties that I just wouldn't be willing to perform. For instance, it seems to be a requirement of the job that all fathers must wear loud pants or a funny fishing hat while doing yard work. I am just barely willing to do yard work at all, and I'll be hanged if I'm going to wear goofy clothes when I do. I also don't believe I could bring myself to be seen in a WORLD'S GREATEST DAD T-shirt or a necktie with tiny images of Foghorn Leghorn patterned across it, even if said articles of clothing were gifts from my children. There's not much I'd not be willing to do for my kids, but awarding them sway over my wardrobe is a sacrifice I am not prepared to make.

Fathers are also expected to cede control of the car radio to their children. This I could not agree to. Though I'd willingly chauffeur my sundry scions to soccer practice, piano lessons, and Cub Scout meetings, I simply refuse to suffer the latest warblings of Britney Spears or 'N Sync while doing so. So perhaps I'm best suited to the role of uncle.

It's an odd thing, this desire to pair up and procreate. Most of us dream of the day that we can be out from under our parents' watchful gaze and away from the stinging barbs and annoying behavior of our siblings, when we can have a place of our own and do what we want when we want. And yet no sooner do we achieve such freedom than we begin scheming to re-create those ties that bind with a whole new group of people, only one of whom we even get to select.

It's probably a good thing that we don't get to select our children, though. I'm not at all certain that my dad would have picked me out of a catalogue. Not that he hasn't always been the most supportive and loving of fathers; he certainly has. In fact, I consider myself to be just about the luckiest son around. But I am not gifted with the traditional traits that most men might look for in a son: I'm inept athletically, I can't build or fix anything (and have no interest in learning), and I'd rather spend a warm summer's day in an air-cooled movie theatre than in the great outdoors. I spent many years being the last one picked on the playground, when teams were culled for pickup games of softball or two-handed touch; I'd hate to think how long I might've waited to be born if families were compiled in the same fashion.

Raising a child seems to me an exceedingly precarious endeavor. It's perhaps a bit like those mosaic kits or paint-by-numbers sets that you see at arts-and-crafts stores. With vigilance and a little luck, you can end up with something to be proud of, that will brighten your life for years to come, but should some little thing go wrong—a passerby bumps your worktable, for example, or you neglect to put on your glasses before sitting down to work—you could end up with a disappointing, botched mess. And one's offspring are less likely to quietly accept being stashed away in the attic than is, say, a poorly executed clown painting.

And fatherhood comes with no guarantees that you will, in the long run, have anything whatsoever in common with your child. A devout, Republican, dog-loving Yankees fan may well be forced to watch with dismay as his son or daughter grows up to be an agnostic Democrat who cheers for the Mets and raises purebred show cats. And there won't be a thing he can do about it.

Still, there's that one day a year when the kids pull the plug on all the squabbling, when you're allowed a steak and all the butter you can stand on that baked potato, when you can fall asleep—belt unbuckled, pants unsnapped—in front of a golf telecast on the tube and not catch grief for it. And that one day just may render it all worthwhile. And for single guys like me, there's always the ballpark, where they'll be giving away free seat cushions to all men of fathering age, no proof of parentage required.

Are You Being Served?

A recent evening found me dining out in the company of ten or twelve friends, most of them women. After the check was presented and everyone had chipped in what they thought they owed, we found ourselves in the unusual predicament of being some forty dollars ahead.

"Give it to the waiter," one woman suggested. "He was cute." Two or three other women agreed with her assessment of his charms and seconded her suggestion. I considered protesting— by now the tip was hovering near the stratospheric level of 40 percent, and I somehow couldn't see that the server had been all that fetching—but I kept mum and gave in. As one who spent more years waiting tables than I care to recall, I have a certain sympathy for servers, who are called upon to pretend to hold in high regard certain patrons who are utterly undeserving of the effort. It's no coincidence that most actors and actresses work in restaurants while seeking their big break; it's a great place to hone one's thespic skills. The server feigns heartfelt concern over our often niggling complaints, and we allow ourselves to be fooled.

When I am being served, I am highly susceptible to the very same tricks of the trade that I relied upon in my days as a waiter. Like my female companions, I too have experienced—and indulged—the impulse to perhaps too generously reward an attractive and attentive female server's efforts, and I suppose it's a sign of progress that women now feel free to be as shallow and superficial as men when awarding gratuities. Over the years I have developed crushes on dozens of waitresses in cafés, coffee bars, and restaurants too numerous to count—women who have served me dinner, brought me a beer, laughed at my jokes, shown interest in my well-being, and, when the time came to say good night, urged me to please return, and soon. Am I kidding myself in believing that these women really found me as charming as they put on? Of course I am, and why not? Such role playing is the very stuff first dates are made of, after all.

And there are so many other services not yet offered to which I would gladly devote my knack for self-deception. For example, I'm never quite so blue as when I step off a plane into the passenger-receiving area of an airport terminal, only to find no familiar face awaiting me. And I doubt that I am alone in this. So I look forward to the day when some savvy entrepreneur begins to market the Airport Sweetheart. One would call the company's headquarters—operators would always be standing by—to create a trip profile, enabling your Airport Sweetheart, once he or she has expressed joy at having you home safe and sound, to ask just the right questions about your journey: How did the sales conference go? Did you enjoy seeing your old friends at the class reunion? Is Great-aunt Matilda feeling better, and was her operation a success? If not, did the reading of the will go to your liking?

The possibilities are endless, and over time and with regular patronage you would find that your Airport Sweetheart, like any other service professional, would come to know your quirks, your likes and dislikes, and those sensitive issues you'd rather not discuss. As for deluding yourself that your Airport Sweetheart really cares a whit one way or the other about your vacation or business trip, don't worry: Self-delusion is a skill like anything else, and practice makes perfect.

Better Living Through Plastics

MY mother is a woman of accomplishments. This is no idle boast; she once shook President Carter's hand, right there under the White House roof. And in the early 1950s she received amorous attention from the King of Western Swing himself, Bob Wills, as he stood on the stage of Oklahoma City's Trianon Ballroom. Oh, sure, it could have been John Kennedy's paw she clasped or Hank Williams who flirted with her; I'll admit those encounters would have made for more impressive tales to tell. Still, I beam with pride whenever I speak of my mom.

And nothing tickles me more than the fact that she, on a warm summer's evening in the early 1960s, hosted a Tupperware party. No single moment in time could more succinctly sum up my childhood than the evening Mom sent my Dad—my pajama-clad siblings and me in tow—off to the drive-in whilst she pitched pie holders and cold-cut containers to women named Madge and Barb.

I love to imagine the scene. While Dad suffered through *Cap-*

tain Sinbad and made countless runs to the concession stand for us kids, Mom greeted, one by one, a string of bouffant-haired, capri-pants-wearing June Cleavers and Laura Petries as they arrived at our home, giddy with anticipation at the chance to see the latest in plastic kitchenware.

I read recently that even today a Tupperware party begins somewhere in the world every three seconds. I get a kick out of imagining housewives in Poland or South Korea or Mozambique thrilling to the sound of that airtight seal for the very first time. In those places these are Tupperware's glory days, a time of promise, of hope and dreams. But have you or anyone you know ever been invited to a Tupperware party? I thought not. Neither have I.

Here in America, Tupperware's promise of a better tomorrow seems to have faded. We are willing now, it seems, to settle for simple utilitarianism where we once dreamed of magic. Oh, sure, Tupperware is still around. For all I know, the company Earl Tupper founded back in 1945 may sell more lettuce crispers and cake savers today than ever before, but the thrill, as the man said, is gone.

Still, I'm pleased to be able to recall those halcyon days of hair spray and Maybelline, of popcorn and a Coke during a double feature at the Skyvue Drive-in, and of young housewives in sundresses listening, rapt, as Mom showed them the way to happiness through fresher, crisper fruits and vegetables.

Flatbed Foolishness

No strain of television commercial comes so close to equaling the low standards set by the American beer industry's insipid propaganda than truck ads. American men, as portrayed in these thirty-second ditties, are utter buffoons, simpletons who require only the basest of activities to keep them happily occupied for hours.

If one would believe the truck industry, no man could hope for more than an afternoon spent driving in mud. Not that I haven't enjoyed mud in my day; as a tot I had no equal in the making of mud pies, and in my adolescent years, I gleefully took part in a number of football games, *après le déluge*. However, now that I am grown to be a man and have put away childish things (well, most of them), it takes more than the spinning of wheels in muck and mire to satisfy me. Call me picky, if you will, but there it is.

The men in truck ads like to hoot, often for no apparent reason. Inspired by nothing more than sliding in behind the wheel of a truck, they shout "Yee-ha!" and "Wa-hoo!" as they rumble off through the brush.

I've driven trucks. My father used to keep a pickup at his place of business, and often, on the summer afternoons of my adolescence, I was dispatched in said vehicle to run one errand or another. I'll not deny that I occasionally relied on expletives to express the discomfort I experienced when forced to sit, while wearing short pants, on that vinyl seat made searingly hot by the relentless Oklahoma sun, but in the interest of propriety, I'll not enumerate here my epithets of choice. Suffice to say, neither "Wa-hoo!" nor "Yee-ha!" was among them.

The names of these vehicles tend to be a bit romanticized, too—consider Range Rover and Pathfinder—but at least I can understand how those handles fit the image the truck manufacturers are pitching. But whose bright idea was it to name a truck Jimmy? What's next? A four-wheel-drive Billy? A vehicle with extra towing power fondly dubbed "The Stevie"?

The men who people these ads all appear to share one craving: the desire to drive somewhere other than the road. They seem to think it a testament to their manhood to be able to drive over a mountain rather than around it. However, I've done a fair amount of traveling around this great land myself, and I didn't find many stretches of road where the terrain these men have such a craving to traverse wasn't fenced in. I suspect the average Joe, who doesn't have a few hundred acres he can call his own, is going to be hard-pressed to find his way off the road and into the not-so-open country. And even if he does manage to somehow escape the asphalt, I suspect he'll find the thrill in negotiating his way through ditches, rocks, and brush to be fleeting at best.

I mean, you're not the Marlboro Man, you bozo. You've got a wife, two kids, and an enlarged prostate, and you're driving a climate-controlled vehicle with a CD changer, surround sound, and Corinthian leather seats. Get your candy ass back out on the interstate.

Mirror, Mirror, on the Wall

O N my dresser stands an inlaid wood frame, which holds a portrait that, judging from its subject's hair and clothes, must surely date from the 1920s. As in many old photos, the age of the woman depicted is difficult to establish. These sepia images offer creatures much like ourselves but somehow not exactly so. This woman wears finery and a corsage at her bosom, so perhaps this sitting occurred on her sweet-sixteenth birthday. Maybe she has just graduated from high school. She may have just been confirmed or have celebrated her bat mitzvah. I acquired the photo in a roundabout fashion and so haven't a clue who the young woman is or what her circumstances were.

I do have this clear idea, though, that someone (and I somehow feel certain it was her parents) dressed this young woman up in fine clothes, adorned her with a silk flower, and stood to the side, beaming with pride, as the photographer captured, for posterity's sake, that now unknowable special moment in the life of their beloved daughter. It's a touching image. One is moved by the pride this couple must have felt for their daughter. To them she must have been the most beautiful girl in the world, and I'm sure they told her as much, and often.

The truth is, bless her heart, the poor thing is, by most standards, a bit plain. Of course, we know, if we've been paying attention at all, that it is not a book's cover that matters but its contents. Still, I find myself musing over what direction this young woman's life took. Did she believe it when her mother told her she was lovely? Or did she, deep down, have an inkling that, barring some ugly-duckling-esque metamorphosis, she was not going to be the belle of any ball and set about, then, to take advantage of her other natural gifts? I like to imagine that she was so rich of heart and soul, so blessed in energy and intelligence, that her looks were unimportant to potential suitors.

After all, precious few of us belong at the head of the class when it comes to appearance. Most of us rely on the fact that we'll be graded on the curve and end up with a C and even maybe a B−. Thankfully, it's a very subjective matter, more inkblot test than true/false quiz. What one person sees in the blot, the next misses entirely.

I'm not sure when I began to sense that I was rather, well, average-looking. I got the requisite positive feedback at home regarding my appearance, but I was no fool: I took that with the grain of salt it called for. A mother is required to dole out such praise, after all; it's in the job description.

I often cringe at scenes in movies and television shows that portray one character or another as grossly unattractive. I wonder how it must feel for an actor to know that he has been cast specifically for his horse face or rotund physique. A person of intelligence can portray a moron, but makeup and costume can do just so much to alter one's appearance; if one is cast as the homely woman or the obese man, one can pretty much assume one fits the bill. One could try to view it as making the best of a difficult situation, I suppose, but it can't be easy for the performer. Surely inside every character actor there hides a leading man or woman yearning to be free.

In a perfect world, each of us would be attractive to the rest of the world one out of every five years. Whether we're tall or short, slim or stout, blond or brunette, whether we have a button nose or a humongous honker, every five years we'd get the opportunity to revel in waves of admiration from the gender of our preference. I could stand a four-year dry spell if I knew that, say, for the duration of 2001, I'd be considered a certified, grade-A hunk. I'd smile with satisfaction as cooing women admired the atrophied tissue I call my biceps, as they furtively sneaked peeks at my utterly pedestrian buttocks, as they gazed longingly into my blue eyes with the dark circles under them. Such a glorious twelve months would make the dreary forty-eight that preceded them worth suffering through. At least we'd all have something to look forward to. With my luck, though, I would finally manage that long-dreamed-of chance of a face-to-face meeting with the lovely and talented Helen Hunt—on New Year's Day, 2002! As usual, a day late, if not a dollar short.

When Animals Attack Bob Saget

THE genre of shockumentaries has begun to spread like crabgrass on an untended lawn. These are those television shows that depict horrific accidents, natural disasters, and animal attacks. Meanwhile the popularity of those *America's Funniest* programs that depict the lighter side of reality seems to be on the wane. These shows offer the wacky mishaps of people who are supposedly just like you and me as they attempt everyday activities like mowing the lawn, grilling a steak, or walking the dog.

We're no longer interested, it seems, in the rib-tickling antics of our fellow citizens; now we prefer to see them swept away by tidal waves, mauled by bears, or caught in the deadly crossfire of a drug bust gone bad. I wonder why that is.

Could it be that things are going too well right now for us Americans? The economy continues to soar, the crime rate is dropping all over the country, we're not at war. So maybe we just need a dash of yin to accompany all that yang, a reminder that—although things are going swimmingly right now—when we least expect it, a tornado could dip down and carry us away, or a roving pack of feral Tasmanian devils could appear to tear us limb from limb.

Or maybe I've got it backward. Maybe these shows offer a sort of reassurance against our fear of disaster. I mean, how many people encounter, in the course of any given year, a Bengal tiger escaped from a local zoo and in search of a snack? I'm guessing one, maybe two tops. So if you viewed a videotape of such an attack, you might feel relieved and say to yourself, "Phew! That's one less thing I have to worry about."

Or maybe we simply require bloody spectacle in our lives. Much as we might like to think we're evolved, that we're more enlightened than our ancestors, are these reality-based programs really any more elevated or edifying than the bearbaiting of Elizabethan England or the public hangings of eighteenth- and nineteenth-century America? Probably not.

I worry that some people will make it their life's goal to somehow appear on one of these programs. I've long suspected that many of the zany "accidents" seen on shows with names like *America's Nuttiest Bloopers and Blunders* were in truth events staged in order to grab a minute or two of prime-time television exposure for those "caught in the act." Achieving fame via a spectacularly staged pratfall is one thing, but risking life and limb by, say, intentionally falling into the crocodile pit at a reptile farm—for the sole purpose of capturing some death-defying footage—is quite another. Still, considering the pervasive fascination that an appearance on television seems to hold for many of us, I wouldn't bet against a few boneheads taking such a chance.

I prefer my reality-based programming to be a bit more practical. I've little interest in programs like *When Animals Get Peckish* or *Mother Nature Miffed*. But I'd make it a point to watch one entitled, "Behind Closed Doors: What Women Really Discuss in the Ladies' Lounge!" In the end, I prefer my reality programming to be educational, not merely alarming.

Getting Personal

E very man, I believe, dreams of living the Lothario's life: a little black book filled with an ever-growing collection of phone numbers; a swanky bachelor pad with lights controlled by dimmers and romantic sambas that fill the room with the flick of a switch; a steady flow of fab femmes I call "Doll" and "Sweetheart." Even as I present myself to the world an enlightened man of the nineties, there's a small part of me that longs to be Peter Lawford, Frank Sinatra, and Dean Martin, circa 1961, all rolled into one.

> **Me:** 5'11", average weight, transplanted Oklahoman, late 30s, writer/editor/new media type, restless mind on permanent road trip (will brake for reptile farms, flea markets, and other fragments of the past), loves Patsy Cline, Tom Waits, and my nieces and nephews. **You:** between 28 and 40, an inquisitive heart, would go see "Carnival of Souls," preferably at a drive-in.

To that end, I decided to place, for the entire month of February, a personal ad in a local publication. Lest you misunderstand, let me state that this was no act of desperation. I did this purely on a lark, with no particular expectations (although I will admit to pricing ice buckets and cocktail glasses at my local Williams-Sonoma outlet and light dimmers at the local hardware emporium).

The first obstacle I faced was composing the ad. I'm not being disingenuous when I say that I've not a clue what my romantic selling points are. After more than twenty years of dating, I'm still not really certain what it is a woman might find attractive about me. I know all the words to "Polka Dots and Moonbeams." I own all thirteen Marx Brothers movies on video. I won a citywide essay contest in the seventh grade. I've voted in every presidential election since 1976. Which of these attributes and accomplishments to include?

I was at a loss and so turned to a few friends, females all, to advise me. Advise me, hell—they wrote the ad for me. It was the smartest thing I could've done; as soon as the ad appeared, the responses started pouring in.

And so it was I learned, once and for all, that I'm not meant for playing the field. More than thirty women responded to my ad. I'd made a vow to myself that I would honor each recipient with at least a phone call, if not a face-to-face meeting. After all, it takes a certain amount of courage to respond to a personal ad, and I felt that such chutzpah should be rewarded. But more than thirty women in four weeks! I'm afraid I found it all a bit overwhelming and threw in the towel after ten or twelve phone calls and a handful of brief meetings.

The problem, I suspect, is that I simply wasn't prepared for such a barrage. I've always been a one-woman man (if that), and expecting myself to be able to suddenly juggle that many women, even over the phone, is a bit like asking an avowed couch potato to set aside his bowl of Cheez Doodles and run the marathon on a moment's notice. He's likely to give up after a few short blocks. It is with a certain regret that I report there were no sparks evident—in either direction, I suspect—during the few in-person encounters in which I indulged; admittedly, this may have heightened my reluctance to continue the race.

Still, I'm not sorry I placed the ad. I chatted on the phone with some terrific women and spent some reasonably pleasant hours in the company of a few others. It's the closest I'll ever come to the Playboy ideal, I'm afraid. Hugh Hefner, it seems, I am not. But in the starry eyes of those responding to my ad, I was the perfect man: sensitive, caring, and loyal, gainfully employed, imbued with senses of both humor and responsibility. And though nothing in the ad suggested it, I'm certain most of them imagined that I possessed the physical charms of Tom Cruise or Tyrone Power or whoever might be their ideal. It's only human nature, after all. We tend to presume blind dates attractive until they're proven homely. So perhaps it was best that I tuckered out early. Though I may have proven a disappointment to the handful of women I met in person, in the mind's eyes of more than two dozen others, I'm still everything they could ever have hoped for in a man. How could I expect to top that?

Learning to Let Go

THOSE who know me well know I'm nothing if not trendy. No one keeps a firmer grip on the zeitgeist than do I. You can imagine my excitement, then, when the well-known multinational conglomerate for whom I'd spent some seventeen months toiling as a Web developer made me an active participant in one of the nation's latest crazes: corporate downsizing. Since I adhere strictly to a one-fad-at-a-time policy, this thoughtful gesture on the part of my former employers saved me the ignominy of joining the local chapter of the Ricky Martin Fan Club.

The truth is, I probably should never have given the ghouls in human resources the opportunity to cut me loose. It's not as if there weren't signs that something wasn't right. My department, once a thriving one with six full-time employees and two interns, had slowly dwindled down to just two of us. My colleagues had somehow seen the writing on the wall and made their escapes. Why had I remained?

I've come to the conclusion that there are two kinds of people: those who cut bait, and those who keep fishing. These two schools are perhaps mostly clearly delineated in the arena of romance.

As one who has experienced both layoffs and breakups, I feel qualified to compare the two experiences. I'm of the opinion that those who would move to greener romantic pastures have plenty to learn from their pinstriped corporate brothers and sisters.

Take, for instance, the moment of truth: the parting of ways. It is common practice, in the business world, to have some unfamiliar face, a complete and total stranger, present when an employee learns he or she is being let go. An excellent strategy, this, one that dissatisfied lovers everywhere should adopt, for the presence of this stranger lowers exponentially the chances that the spurned party will openly weep. I know that, had my most recent ex made it a point to have her mother, say, or Stanislaus, her super, present when she revealed her deeply felt aversion to ever seeing me again, I very likely would have made it through her door and out of her building under my own power. I still shudder when I recall the scene—me in a heap on her floor, holding on for dear life to the leg of her sofa until she pried my fingers loose, picked me up, threw me over her shoulder, and carried me to the curb, where I laid sobbing for an hour and a half, all the while calling out for Petey, the stuffed bear I lost in kindergarten.

Severance pay and the extension of benefits are corporate practices that, with a little adapting, could also serve those cruelly thrust into the dark night of solitude that is the single life. If one could turn, in a pinch, to one's recent significant other for the same comforts he or she recently supplied so willingly, it might make for an easier transition.

Perhaps federal legislation should be drafted that requires the jilter to offer the jilted extended romantic benefits, like the COBRA plan, which continues medical coverage for the newly unemployed. Sure, it would come at a dear price (there would be no more dutch treat), but if one were willing to spring for dinner or perhaps an evening at the movies, with popcorn, Twizzlers, and a large soft drink thrown in, one could enjoy the delight of hearing one's former partner again laughing at one's jokes, the calm of once again being reassured that there's nothing odd about owning fourteen pairs of underwear with Luke Skywalker and Darth Vader on them. If one were able to swing a higher premium, one could even take advantage of the full benefits plan, which would include conjugal visits. One caveat, though: As with an HMO physician forced to treat a nosebleed even as his tee time approaches, it's likely one's provider would be less than enthusiastic about fulfilling this benefit.

So, should a federal statute protecting the no-longer-loved one day come to pass, my advice is that you pass on the full benefits plan and apply the money saved toward the purchase of a dog. This will afford you a relationship that, while lacking in conjugal benefits, boasts a constancy and longevity you might never find in a romantic coupling.

Is My Watch Fast?

I'M not certain exactly when it occurred, but at some point in my life I became acutely—even painfully—aware of how quickly time flies. I suspect it was upon the occasion of my twenty-ninth birthday, the first birthday about which I had even remotely mixed feelings. I had theretofore placed the annual festival of my genesis just a notch below Christmas on the list of Days to Be Fervently Anticipated, but as I stood on the brink of my thirties, I was amazed and not a little alarmed at how quickly the carefree decade that was my twenties had whizzed by.

Things didn't slow a bit as I zipped through my thirties. In fact, someone seems to have stepped on the gas. It's as if my life, once a winding country lane leading who knew where, has merged into a superhighway. I am forced to hurtle ever faster toward my final destination, with nary a rest stop or a Stuckey's in sight.

One rather odd side effect to this heightened sense of tenure-awareness is akin to the young Alvy Singer's reaction, in Woody

Allen's *Annie Hall,* to the news that the ever-expanding universe will, in several million years, explode: He stops doing his homework. "What's the point?" he wonders.

What's the point indeed? It's a question I ask myself when I think of our society's obsession with home ownership. I have never owned a home and can easily see myself never doing so. People pay for homes over thirty years, for heaven's sake. A person my age who buys a home won't be free and clear until he or she hits seventy! If this hypothetical individual is male, he'll likely have the luxury of living in a paid-for dwelling for all of seven years before he kicks the bucket (if the actuarial tables are to be believed).

If one had a legitimate shot at living, say, 150 years, devoting 30 of them to paying off a mortgage might seem a worthwhile endeavor. Many of us, it seems, make decisions on the assumption that we're going to live a long life, but I'm here to tell you that that's not true. You may live to be ninety, but you'll get there and you'll wonder where the years went. I already do that, and I'm only forty-two.

And yet, I think what's important is not only how long one lives but when one lives. Let's face it, some periods in history are simply more interesting than others. Take, for example, my late great-grandmother's life span. Born in Iowa, she moved to what was then Oklahoma Territory at the age of sixteen. Her family made the trek in a covered wagon. And yet Great-grandmother Oakes lived long enough to see the invention of the automobile, the telephone, electric lights, radio, movies, and television. She saw men walk on the moon. In her youth, the marches of John Philip Sousa were all the rage, and before she died the Beatles had come and gone. Things have moved more quickly in the past century than in any period in history. Progress used to come so slowly that the discovery of bronze was given its own age, some two thousand years long!

The only fear I have about death is that I'll just miss out on something good. Perhaps they'll finally make jet packs available to us, and we'll be able to fly to work. Maybe compact discs will become affordably priced. Or, with my luck, a cure will be discovered for the very ailment that brought on my demise—the day after I'm gone.

Much Ado About Nothing

HAVE you heard the news? It's not likely you could've missed the announcements. The folks in Golden, Colorado, are literally shouting it from the mountaintops: Coors Light now comes in widemouthed cans! I can only ask: Is there a poor soul anywhere to be found who leads an existence so dismal, so dreary, that this news brightens his day?

Adolph's people claim that their new can offers a smoother pour, which, of course, raises the question: Who's been having difficulty pouring beer? I've been dispensing the stuff, either into a glass or down my gullet, for more than twenty years now, and I've rarely spilled a drop.

Of course, it's not only the Coors company that resorts to such tactics. They're just carrying on a long and storied advertising tradition of making much ado about nothing. Take the "smaller is better" school of product design. People were paid (and handsomely, I'm guessing) to come up with such products as Mini M&M's, Ritz Bits, and Butterfinger BBs. You see, they're exactly like a regular Butterfinger, only *smaller*! Get it? Well, just in case you don't, an extensive ad campaign, costing millions, has been launched. But are the people at Nestlé so bereft of inspiration that they couldn't concoct a new variety of candy bar? Were they forced to settle for resizing an old one?

Companies who peddle paper goods trumpet the addition of adorable little icons to the edges of their paper towels as if this amounts to a design breakthrough. In the ads, it always seems to be a female homemaker who is thrilled by this development, but can there possibly exist anywhere a harried housewife who, in her haste to sop up Junior's regurgitated baby formula from her sweater or Rover's backyard droppings from her shoe, pauses first to admire the pink daisies or blue teddy bears on her paper towel? Of course not. If ever a product was utilitarian—not decorative—in nature, it's the paper towel, and why pretend otherwise?

Imagine if those we strive daily to impress were as easily satisfied as the advertisers think we, the consuming public, must be. Suppose your supervisor at work recommended you for a big promotion simply because you'd taught yourself to count to ten in Spanish. Would you consider touting, in bold print at the very top of your résumé, that you're expert in the proper handling of a pair of scissors and can stay inside the lines when using crayons? Try impressing a prospective paramour with your newly improved VCR-programming skills, and see how far it gets you.

No, most of us are held to a higher set of standards. So I'm wondering if perhaps there is not a potential market for ad agencies to shill for individuals. I could certainly use someone to make a mountain out of my molehill: "The new, improved Brett Leveridge: 10 percent fewer split infinitives than before!"

Sunday in the Park with Me

Arbor Day is one nationally observed holiday that doesn't really speak to the average New Yorker. Many a tourist, upon visiting New York City for the first time, laments the lack of chlorophyll. "Where," Herb from St. Paul asks, "are the trees?" "There's no grass," exclaims Dot from Chattanooga. "There are no lawns!" True enough, Dot and Herb, we New Yorkers do have to get by without much in the way of foliage, but I, for one, enter this in the credits column, not the debits. For where there are no trees, there is no raking of leaves. Where there are no shrubs, there is no trimming to be done. No lawns means no mowing, no edging, no fertilizing, watering, or weeding, no cute plaster deer or lawn jockeys. And that's just fine with me.

New Yorkers take comfort in the knowledge that their flora fix lies just a short stroll (or subway ride) away. Of course, there are many spots in Manhattan for which the term *park* is something of a misnomer. Most don't consider a small patch of cracked and buckled concrete dotted with a handful of benches in varying states of disrepair a park, but fortunately these little neighborhood offerings are not the only game in town. The roll call of worthy urban oases in Manhattan alone (not even considering the other four boroughs) includes that long-standing bastion of bohemia, Washington Square Park; the Upper West Side's long and lovely Riverside Park; and even—though I rarely make it to that neighborhood—the Upper East Side's Carl Schurz Park, at the northern end of which sits Gracie Mansion, the perpetual home of Gotham's mayor.

But the grandest common of them all is Central Park, an expansive exhibition of flora and fauna (particularly of the *homo sapiens* variety) that never ceases to delight. Any tourist who visits the Big Apple and doesn't spend the better part of a Saturday or Sunday afternoon enjoying Central Park hasn't, in my view, really experienced New York.

But for me the park's charm has little to do with its greenery; it's the people, not the plants, that draw me. Not long ago I was Rollerblading midpark in front of the Naumberg bandshell. A man in his thirties hefted a little girl I took to be his daughter up onto the stage and proclaimed loudly, in stentorian tones, "Ladies and gentlemen, all the way from North Carolina—Miss Victoria Stafford!" The wide-eyed little girl stood there for a moment or two until, suddenly overcome by shyness, she ran into the man's arms, burying her face in his shoulder. I was surprised—and more than a little pleased—when that crowd of seen-it-all New Yorkers, with grins on their faces, gave it up for that little girl, awarding her a healthy round of applause.

Now, if Dad had opted to orchestrate his daughter's public debut on the subway, say, or during rush hour in Grand Central

Station, I suspect Miss Stafford's reception would have been a little less enthusiastic, but the joyous denizens of Central Park were more than welcoming.

In one stroll through the park, I've encountered a troupe of percussionists, a whole range of jazz combos playing everything from bebop to fusion, jugglers, stilt walkers, Brazilian capoeira artists engaged in their ultrachoreographed battles accompanied by the tinkling of berembau, Pavarotti performing for a hundred thousand of his closest friends, and Kevin Kline emoting in *Measure for Measure*. I even met the Katie Couric of Turkey, a woman who is a huge star in her homeland. She's a model, an actress, and an anchorwoman on Turkey's CNN franchise. She gets mobbed by fans on the streets of Ankara but goes largely unrecognized here. Maybe I should have walked her over to the bandshell and introduced her to Manhattan; then again, maybe not.

The Dusty Road to Stardom

THIS life we lead offers some odd twists and turns, does it not? It often places us in situations we might never have imagined for ourselves.

So it was that I found myself onstage before a packed house at Fez, a nightspot on Manhattan's Lower East Side, an un-likely—but not unhopeful—contestant in a Dusty Springfield look-alike contest.

The occasion was the latest Loser's Lounge, an approximately monthly series of tributes to various pop-music icons from the sixties and seventies. The house band, the Kustard Kings, plays behind an ever-varying lineup of downtown performers who stop by to warble a tune identified with that night's honoree. Past subjects have ranged from Neil Diamond to Elton John, from Carole King to Burt Bacharach, but on this night homage was being paid to the late, great queen of blue-eyed soul, Dusty Springfield. Following the second of the evening's three sets, the Dusty look-alike contest was held. The top prize was a three-disc Springfield boxed set, and there were four additional prizes of single-disc samplers taken from that collection.

Prizes worth coveting, there's no doubt, but I am not, at first glance, someone who might be considered a suitable entrant: Dusty Springfield was a blonde (I'm brunette) and eschewed facial hair (I sport a goatee). Oh, and there's the fact that she was a woman (I am a man).

But the contest was off to a slow start: Only a pair of entrants had stepped onstage, and when the emcee announced that there were no gender restrictions on contestants, I thought, what the heck.

I expected to get a good laugh from the crowd as I stepped into the spotlight, and so I did. Really, that should have been reward enough, but I found myself coveting one of those CDs. I didn't expect to win the contest, but surely, on the novelty factor alone, I could snag a runner-up spot. But soon four more women and one more man each got up the nerve to enter the contest. Even the gender-novelty factor, once so firmly in my favor, was now split between me and this interloper.

What I didn't know was that this was no mere popularity contest; there were three different categories in which the eight contestants were to be judged. The first: Appearance, with special attention paid to hair color (Strike one!), eyeliner (Strike two!), and gown (You're out!). But this was not, we had been assured by the emcee, a mere look-alike competition but also a Dusty *feel-alike* contest. So my hopes, faint as they were, lay in the latter two categories: Emotion and Poise.

For the former, each contestant was to step up to the mike and recite the title of the hit song Springfield recorded with the

Pet Shop Boys in 1987: "What Have I Done to Deserve This?" I watched as the two entrants preceding me did a semitank on their delivery, and fearing that this might be my one good chance to make a favorable impression on the judges, I gave it everything I had, summoning up all the pain, disappointment, and disillusionment that ever I've suffered. I even threw in a pregnant pause worthy of a soap opera star for additional dramatic effect.

Stepping away from the mike and back to the chorus line of contestants, I felt good; I'd done my best. The emcee quipped, "Well, it looks as though someone took acting classes in junior college." (Little did he know how right he was: I have a B.F.A. in theatre.)

And painful memories from those acting classes were soon to come back to haunt me. For the final category, we were asked to exhibit poise as we left the stage by posing à la Agnes Moorehead's Endora on the old *Bewitched* television show. Remember that thing she did with her hands whenever she disappeared in a huff or put a spell on Durwood? That's the sort of gesture they were looking for, and I can't deny that I choked. My mind was a total blank. I froze just as I used to freeze during improv exercises in those acting classes of yore. A mere few moments on that stage became for me a near eternity of torment. I wracked my brain trying to gain the inspiration to strike even the feeblest of poses, but if my life had depended on it, I could not have done so. I finally realized it was not to be and slinked off the stage in shame.

Of course, as the prizes were about to be announced, I held out hope that somehow my performance in the second category might be enough to carry me. Or that perhaps the judges would give me credit for having had the nerve to be the first male to enter the competition.

But alas, the fourth, third, second, and first runners-up were all announced, and my name was not among them.

I won't deny my disappointment at losing, but I've lost before and survived and shall do so again. Just as I turned my back on the gridiron, many years ago, when I realized that I was likely to spend most of my time warming the bench, so have I now turned my back on look-alike contests devoted to blond female pop stars of the 1960s. But I have not given up; I shall continue to endeavor to find *something* at which I can excel. All suggestions are welcome.

See You in September

I spend every Labor Day gritting my teeth as op-ed columnists and on-air commentators bemoan the passing of another summer as if they are expressing a universal sorrow. At times like this I feel like a Unitarian enduring a fire-and-brimstone fundamentalist sermon: Though I may concur with certain of the preacher's points, I can't help but feel that he's overstating his case.

For unless you're at the beach or poolside—and let's face it, at any given time, what percentage of us are?—summer is surely the most overrated annual event this side of New Year's Eve. The joys of the season are largely mythical. For many, the word *summer* conjures images of sun, sand, and surf, of long, lazy days spent idling in a hammock, of cookouts, pool parties, and miniature golf. All of which admittedly sound delightful, but whose docket is so clear? Unless you're under the age of sixteen or make your living as a teacher, your boss, like mine, probably expects you at the office eight hours a day, five days a week—

even in June, July, and August—and would consider "But . . . *it's summer!*" an unacceptable explanation for a prolonged absence.

No, that vision of summer is largely a pipe dream, but I'm happy to remind you of some of the season's attributes that are not: searingly hot vinyl car seats, clothes that stick to one's damp skin, and yard work. This last is reason enough to resent the onset of summer and is perhaps the primary motivation for my immigration, all those years ago, from the suburbs of Oklahoma City to the island of Manhattan. Not that this concrete jungle is any kind of summer paradise; it's hot, hazy, and humid. But at least it doesn't need mowing.

Autumn, on the other hand, is a grand time to be in Gotham. In autumn the city is imbued with the sort of glow usually seen only in the work of a master cinematographer. The haze dissipates, there's a nip in the air, and the island's energy, once sapped by the summer heat, returns with a flourish, like a leggy supermodel just back from the Hamptons.

It's been suggested to me on more than one occasion—and by members of more than one gender—that summer's tribulations are worth enduring if only for the expanses of skin that are bared for our pleasure; even this, I submit, is a mixed blessing at best. Let's face it, it's a relatively rare human being who possesses a midriff or a set of gams worthy of display. Most of us look far better in a sweater and slacks than we ever would in a cut-off T-shirt and bikini briefs. The good Lord has blessed each of us with a perfectly good imagination; pray, let us give each other occasion to exercise it.

Perhaps the biggest trial summer presents us is olfactory in nature. Yes, there are pleasant smells associated with the season:

the sweet scent of a perfectly ripe peach, the alluring aroma of steaks on the grill, the wafting delights of honeysuckle in the air. But summer is decidedly unkind to many of nature's creatures. Late some August afternoon, stand close and take a good whiff of your dog, your eight-year-old, or your next-door neighbor. Chances are, all three are in dire need of a good scrubbing, and none is likely to undertake it on his own.

So decry the passing of summer if you must, but be aware that the sentiment is not universal, that there are others like me whose hearts are set aloft by the delights of autumn—by shopping for new school clothes, sampling the season's first pumpkin pie, or indulging in a long stroll on a chill night with just a hint of wood smoke in the air. And we fallophiles will no longer remain silent. We will loudly celebrate our seasonal preferences with energy, enthusiasm, and pride—autumnal pride.

On Being a Marked Man

 **M**ANY readers will have, at this point in the book, gained a pretty good sense of the wholesome, rather insulated environment in which I grew to adulthood. I often crack that I grew up on *Leave It to Beaver,* and it's only a half joke. Mom didn't wear pearls when waxing the floors, but otherwise my childhood wasn't so very different from Wally and the Beav's.

Conspicuous by their absence from my own private Mayfield were tattoos. The only one I recall encountering adorned the arm of my fifth-grade Little League coach. His name has escaped the rather feeble clutches of my memory, but I clearly recall his essence, his look. Tall and lanky, like Sam Shepard, he was a truck driver possessed of a truck driver's deep tan. He smoked cigarettes. He told off-color jokes, used words I couldn't always define but didn't dare repeat. And his tattoo was a daunting one: a

buxom, ebon-haired bathing beauty sans bathing suit, perpetu-
ally coiled in a seductive pose right there on his left arm. She was
perhaps the first naked lady I ever encountered, and she remains,
to this day, one of the most impressive.

Tattoos, to my young mind, were outward shows of ma-
chismo, personal banners of worldliness acquired in exotic,
dangerous places like Singaporean ports of call and Mexican
border towns. Sailors had them, drifters, ex-cons. Not that it occurred to me to try, but in my youth I would have had difficulty,
I know, reconciling a tattoo with, say, membership in the honor
society. One could have a tattoo, or one could get straight As.
Surely it wasn't possible to do both, was it?

More than a decade spent in New York has slowly altered my
perception of this age-old body art. Here tattoos are found on
hipsters, Hell's Angels, homebodies, hicks, harlots, highbrows,
and the hoi polloi. One of the loves of my life was tattooed, and
don't think that didn't shake me up a little. Believe me, that boy
back in Oklahoma would never have guessed that he'd one day
date a marked woman. But I fell hard for a nice girl from Iowa,
and damned if she didn't have a lunar tableau etched right there
above her right shoulder blade!

So it was that I slowly came to consider taking the plunge
myself. For some time I toyed with the notion of marking my
arm with a Route 66 highway shield. It wasn't a matter of decid-
ing I wanted a tattoo and then having to choose an image. The
image came first; it's the only one I ever considered.

The tricky part is that, until recently, tattooing was illegal in
New York City. Of course, there's a law against jaywalking, too,
but one is not likely to do hard time for it. The NYPD has more

than enough to keep them busy without concerning themselves with these lesser offenses, so even when they, strictly speaking, were prohibited, tattoo parlors still thrived.

"Cool skates, dude!" Clay, the young tattoo artist, exclaimed, as I entered the East Village tattoo parlor, in-line skates in hand. He sat me down, showed me his portfolio, and told me he'd happily answer any questions I might have. This reception was, I must admit, a pleasant surprise. My inner dork had half expected to be greeted with derision, labeled a poseur, and quickly shown the door.

I had a moment, too, of insecurity regarding my choice of body graphic. The work displayed in Clay's portfolio was a little more, well, extreme than my tame little highway sign. Here were monsters, flaming skulls, dragons, skeletons—the stuff nightmares are made of. Would he find my little icon too dull? Would he decline my business or, worse, try to spice my design up a bit once he had me marked, perhaps wrap a hissing viper around my Route 66 shield?

I told Clay what I had in mind, and he seemed enthusiastic enough, allaying my fears. We scheduled an appointment for the following Monday afternoon, which allowed three full days for the inevitable second thoughts to arise.

Oddly, though, the doubts never really gained a foothold. I'd mulled so long over this decision that now that the time was near, I didn't waffle. I wasn't particularly apprehensive upon my return to East Second Street, though I didn't relish the pain I expected to undergo. Upon my arrival I gave Clay the artwork, and he disappeared into the rear of the parlor, using a machine to turn the graphic into a stencil that would be transferred onto

my upper arm, serving as his guide as he did the actual tattooing. I waited in the lobby, trying to ignore the incessant, whin-
ing buzz emitting from some recess of the parlor.

Thankfully, that unseen recipient was not shrieking in agony
or I might have suddenly recalled an urgent appointment and
fled the premises. Instead, I passed the time flipping through a
stack of tattoo magazines. These were not reassuring, however.
These publications, which seem to cater to the more devout
among the tattoo faithful, served to raise a few last-minute
doubts in my mind. It occurred to me, after paging through two
or three issues, that I hadn't seen a single individual on those
something-less-than-glossy pages with whom I'd feel comfortable having dinner. Was I about to join a club of which I didn't
really want to be a member? What I wouldn't have given for a
well-worn *People* magazine right about then.

Just then Clay reappeared, perhaps sensing my sudden lack
of resolve, and ushered me back to his workspace. It was a tiny
cubicle, not unlike an examination room in a clinic though dif-
fering distinctly in décor from any doctor's office I've seen. He
shaved my upper arm, applied the stencil, had me examine it in
a mirror to ensure it was placed just so, and cranked up his in-
strument of torture.

Actually, I'm being a bit dramatic. The pain involved was sig-
nificantly less than I'd expected. It felt a bit like someone with
long nails giving me a good, hard scratch. It hurt, yes, but it was
not excruciating; I didn't even whimper.

In little more than a quarter of an hour Clay completed his
work. The tattoo looked great, exactly like the original I'd presented to him during our initial consultation. We discussed the

first week's care for the tattoo (plenty of Neosporin), I handed Clay his seventy-five bucks, and I was on my way.

Since that day, I've experienced the occasional pang of doubt. Did I do the right thing? Will I regret having this done? I truly don't think so. I'm really rather pleased with it. Clay told me I'd likely return someday for another tattoo. He said that most people, having survived the harrowing experience of their first tattoo, return for another. I can understand this phenomenon, but I suspect this will be it for me. This tattoo is a form of tribute, to the road, the legend that is Route 66. It's a reminder of my 1992 cross-country trip. And to some degree, I suppose, if I'm truly honest, it's my own rather mild (and belated) form of rebellion. I don't think another is in the cards.

Don't Believe the Hype

I have no statistics to back me up, but I am convinced that Thanksgiving is the most popular of all our national celebrations. And that seems only right; after all, it's a holiday that each of us—the devout and the doubtful—can celebrate. We can all agree that we are a blessed nation, with much for which to be grateful, even if we can't quite agree upon which entity should rightfully be thanked.

In fact, Thanksgiving may well be as close as we'll ever come to achieving a perfect holiday. It comes with no gift-giving angst, no cards to be sent, no parties to be planned. It's an opportunity to gather in the warmth of one's family and friends, to savor—and give thanks for—the many blessings that we tend to take for granted the other 364 days of the year.

Still, I will admit to one qualm regarding even this most elevated and edifying of national observances. I'm not at all comfortable with the cult of turkey that has arisen around that final Thursday of each November.

I mean, c'mon—*turkey*? Not that I advocate outlawing this rather feeble fowl, but there's little to be said on its behalf. At best it can be described as having an inoffensive taste, but then, it is barely a taste at all.

Turkey is like the hardworking but largely ineffectual utility infielder at the end of the bench who bats only .176, the guy to whom a baseball manager turns only once or twice a season, in a game that has gone deep into extra innings, when there's simply no one else left to pinch-hit. Turkey, like that ballplayer, is admittedly better than nothing, but by just a hair's breadth.

I have a feeling that turkey was the featured dish at the first Thanksgiving not because the Pilgrims and their Native American neighbors were so terribly fond of it but simply because their choices were limited. Had turkey faced competition, on that inaugural Thanksgiving Day buffet table, from prime rib of beef, grilled salmon, or even a pepperoni pizza, I'm guessing that bland bird would have placed a distant fourth. Those Pilgrims would've been eating leftover turkey sandwiches for weeks.

Which is exactly how turkey was meant to be enjoyed, of course; the quintessential team player, it goes best between two thick slices of rye bread and accompanied by lettuce, tomato, Swiss cheese, and a swipe of spicy mustard.

The true MVP of the Thanksgiving lineup—if I may extend my sports metaphor just a bit further—is, of course, pumpkin pie. Here is a reason to be thankful. As far as I'm concerned, Thanksgiving dinner should begin and end with this delectable treat, but in what I suspect is a holdover from our Puritan heritage, it seems we cannot allow ourselves to indulge in such gustatory delight until we've earned it by suffering through a couple of helpings of the dry, bland fowl.

And yet I must admit that most of us, and I include myself here, have more in common with Tom Turkey than we might care to admit: Our dreams may be grand, but our lives are workaday. We are steady and reliable but rarely manage anything more glamorous than clothing, housing, and feeding ourselves and those we care for. So perhaps it is fitting, on a day that we pause to give thanks for those same creature comforts, that we elevate the turkey from his lowly position. Perhaps by glorifying the turkey, we are, in roundabout fashion, praising Joe and Jane American, the unsung people who keep this country running.

Or maybe that's just the tryptophan talking.

How I Learned to Stop Worrying and Love the Massage

For my birthday, my friend William presented me with a gift certificate good for a ninety-minute massage at a swanky spa in midtown Manhattan. This thoughtful gift brought with it more anxiety than anticipation, however, as I am just not very comfortable in the role of client. I try to let my money do the talking, but I usually end up going to great lengths to ensure that the people whom I hire to perform services . . . well, *like* me.

For example, before an appointment with my hairstylist, I always wash my hair, even though I know that a shampoo is part of the package for which I'm paying. I worry that people will think I make a practice of walking around with hair that is less than squeaky clean. And although I've never enlisted the services of a professional house cleaner, I know that if I did, I'd spend hours preparing for each visit, dusting, vacuuming, wiping, and straightening up. Oh, I'd be very careful not to get the place *too* clean, so as not to tip my hand, but heaven forbid a stranger, even one I'm paying a pretty penny, should discover what a slob I am.

Having never experienced a professional massage, I was clueless as to the proper etiquette and procedures. What if I took off too many clothes? My masseuse might then think me a rube or, worse, an aggressive oaf. And frankly, I was somewhat apprehensive about revealing my naked self to a stranger. I couldn't help but fear her unspoken assessment. Not that I'm completely unattractive, mind you, but what if her previous client was a totally buff Adonis? Could she refrain from giggling as she worked on my chicken legs, my skinny arms, my small but undeniable love handles?

Don't get me wrong; I knew it was to be a massage, not an evening of lovemaking. I was fully aware that I'd be dealing with a trained massage therapist, a health care professional who'd gone through months of strenuous and thorough training. Hers was to perform a therapeutic service for a fee, not to rate me on a scale of 1 to 10.

And yet, I was to be alone with a woman, naked (or nearly so), and in a supine position. That's not something I've experienced so often that I can be cavalier about it.

All of which leads to the key issue, the one that all men who would be massaged must face: the unwelcome and inappropriate erection. It's an odd sort of turnabout, when you think about it. Usually, when one is alone and naked with a woman, the erection is an agreeable development, but during a massage, it is clearly to be avoided if at all possible. What is to be done if this uncomfortable situation does happen to, er, arise? Should one apologize? Excuse oneself and hurriedly return to the locker room for a cold shower? Pretend it's not there? Talk a little baseball?

So why must it be a woman, you might ask. Why not book an appointment with a masseur instead? Well, if I'm concerned about an unexpected woody in the presence of a woman, imagine the can of worms that might be opened should tumescence come calling while I, happily heterosexual, am being massaged by a man. That could be a life-altering experience.

For six months I waffled. My gift certificate was on the verge of expiring when William began to nudge me, making sure I didn't let it go to waste. Finally, I picked up the phone, dialed the number, and made an appointment for the following Tuesday afternoon. My massage was to be administered by Priscilla.

At William's suggestion, I arrived early so as to take full advantage of the spa's facilities, the sauna and steam room. Never one to spend much time in gyms or health clubs, I've had precious little experience with these mini-Hades, and I have to say I'm not sure I get the attraction. The steam room reminded me of nothing so much as a New York City subway platform on a muggy August afternoon. I found myself wishing I were home, basking in the frosty output of my air conditioner.

To make matters worse, I picked up a spray bottle, thinking a little cool water in the face might prove refreshing. Unfortunately, the bottle didn't contain water; it was eucalyptus juice. When finally the stinging in my eyes began to lessen, I realized I was out of my element.

The good news was that William, who is himself a massage therapist at the spa, had a break between clients and looked me up, just as my vision was returning to normal. He took me under his wing, showed me where the robes were kept, and tipped me off that the spa even offered jockstraps for the shyer among their clientele. This went a long way toward alleviating my fears. Keeping my boys in a nice snug bundle would surely help should too much of my blood begin to collect in one particular region.

After perhaps the most thorough shower I've ever subjected myself to (who knew what nook or cranny Priscilla might explore as she worked me over?), I donned the impressively thick and absorbent robe and waited, in a lounge designed for that purpose, for Priscilla to summon me. Two fiftyish women in robes that matched mine were there, chatting at length about their favorite methods of conquering heel calluses. One was a loofah devotee, while the other took a razor blade (!) to hers, just after bathing. They barely acknowledged me, which is probably just as well, as I had little to add to that discussion.

Finally, from behind me, a voice said, "Brett?" I rose and was greeted by a pleasant smile and a warm handshake; Priscilla had a nice strong grip. I felt better already.

I followed her into a small room, where she asked me if this was my first visit to the spa. It was, I answered. And was this my first massage? Upon learning that it was, she lit up with enthusiasm. "Oh, I just love giving people their first massage! I remember my first one so well. When it was over, I wondered why I'd ever waited so long!" She explained that, as I was a man, she'd limit herself to the areas north of my naval and south of my midthigh. This was, of course, fine with me, as it was the region between those two points that was the primary cause of my anxiety, jockstrap or no.

Priscilla instructed me to remove the robe and lie on my back on the padded massage table, with the light cotton blanket that lay folded on the table draped over me. She left the room while I did as she asked, and upon her return, she dimmed the already soft peach-colored lighting. This was to be an aromatherapy massage, and she asked what kind of results I desired: Did I want a massage that would leave me relaxed, one that would send me back out into the world feeling invigorated, perhaps one that would be good for my kidneys? (I'm kicking myself for not asking for specifics on that one.) I opted for a relaxed state, and she offered, one by one, five different scented oils for my consideration. I lay there in the darkened room, wearing nothing but a jockstrap, covered with a blanket, while a woman I'd only just met waved vials of essential oils under my nostrils. And yet, Priscilla's friendly, professional manner had put me largely at ease.

I decided upon the first scent offered (lavender, I was to later learn). Four of the five oils smelled pleasant enough; the fifth brought to mind cottage cheese two weeks past its expiration date, but I kept that to myself. Priscilla explained that I would remain covered by the blanket throughout the session, that she'd uncover an arm or leg when the time came to work on it. Somehow, I'd imagined the kneading occurring while I was buck naked and exposed, so what little anxiety I had left melted away. By now I felt so comfortable I began to grow sleepy, what with my recumbent position, the comfy blanket, the soft lighting, the ambient Vivaldi.

I perked right up, however, as Priscilla began the session with facial shiatsu. Much of my tension is stored in my face, so those so-good-it-hurts waves of sensation instantly brought me into the here and now.

I was intrigued to find that some of the areas I expected to be especially sensitive (my shoulders and neck, for example, where I constantly experience tension) didn't generate extreme pain, while seemingly harmless areas like my forearms yielded intense discomfort under the pressure of Priscilla's powerful grip. She urged me not to allow myself to drift off to sleep, as this was my first massage and she didn't want me to miss a moment of it, but she needn't have worried; there was enough pain mixed in with the relaxing pleasure to ensure that I didn't doze off.

She worked all the promised areas of my body from the top of my head to the tips of my toes. I was a bit surprised that I experienced perhaps the greatest pleasure and release as she gently worked on my hands. My hands, of all things—who knew?

At massage's end, I would gladly have lined up for seconds. All my concerns had been unfounded, all my apprehensions baseless. It was sheer delight. I should never have waited so long to redeem the gift certificate; I hope too much time doesn't pass before I can treat myself to another afternoon spent under Priscilla's ministrations. And this I vow: Next time, there'll be no guilt, no fear!

My Dinner with Charla

I'M seated at a cozy corner table in the City Diner, a 1950s-themed restaurant in Weatherford, Oklahoma, having just ordered, with an appropriately crimson face, the "Ooby Dooby," a chicken-breast sandwich with barbecue sauce. I usually observe a strict boycott of such theme restaurants, but tonight I'm willing to bend my rules. The restaurant, you see, was selected by my dining companion, Charla Hahn.

This name probably means nothing to you, gentle reader, but it has, since the time I passed from childhood to adolescence, been one of great resonance to me. For four years I worshipped Charla Hahn from afar, and in this I don't think I was alone. I'm willing to bet that most of the awkward young men who attended junior high and high school with Charla felt very much as I did.

Charla was the girl next door of girls next door, the Mother of All Homecoming Queens, managing to be at once utterly wholesome and sexy as hell, a cheerleader with sandy blond hair, blue-gray eyes, and a smile that made your knees buckle. She was totally out of my league on my best day and, to top it off, two years ahead of me in school. And let's face it, no gap in the world is less likely to be bridged than the one that exists between an attractive girl in the ninth grade and an adoring dork in the seventh. I knew this even then, as well as I knew my own name. Only fourteen years old when first I became aware of her, Charla might just as well have been thirty. Of course that two-year age gap, once so daunting, is now meaningless; today Charla and I are, for all intents and purposes, the same age. And here I am, some twenty-five years after I first encountered her, finally enjoying a dinner for two in her company. God is in his heaven and all is right with the world, for those blue eyes still shine as brightly as ever; that smile still sparkles.

As does, alas, the stone on Charla's left ring finger. Though I wish I could tell you that she'd waited for me all these years, the truth is, Charla's name is no longer Hahn. She's been married, and happily so, for years. She and her husband, Mike, are the proud parents of three terrific kids. One may wonder why, then, since I knew all this before I contacted her, I bothered to look Charla up and invite her to dinner. Call it a lark—a sop, perhaps, to that dorky kid who would have been thrilled to learn that one day he'd be dining alone with Charla, even all these years—and kids—later.

And in many ways this is an old-fashioned date, one that evokes those awkward adolescent evenings of my high school years. Having flown home to Oklahoma City for the holidays, I am forced to borrow my father's car, just like in the old days. I pick Charla up at her home, where I am obliged to meet her family (although it is her husband, not her father, who gives me the once-over). I even open the car door for her and struggle, as in days gone by, to make small talk on the way to the restaurant. For a brief moment, I silently chastise myself for having the gall to think I can pull this off. That's Charla Hahn sitting next to me! What the hell am I thinking?! Fortunately, once we are seated in a booth at the City Diner, conversation flows easily, and my confidence, such as it is, returns.

Charla and I have precious little catching up to do. The truth is, we have limited shared history. We lived, for most of those years we attended school together, in parallel universes. She hadn't even known I existed, I don't believe, until we shared a geometry class in my sophomore—her senior—year. And even after that, our relationship was limited to exchanged pleasantries as we took our seats in Mr. Blackmon's classroom and perhaps a smile and a quick wave when we encountered each other in the hallway between classes.

Now I want to have a conversation with Charla that we would never have held back then. Although I was smart, well liked for the most part, and considered funny by most of my friends, I wasn't terribly good-looking and was noticeably lacking in athletic prowess—a guy's one sure ticket to influence and popularity. So while everyone knew who Charla Hahn was, only people who came in direct contact with me—teachers, classmates, and such—knew of Brett Leveridge. I wondered if that was such a bad thing. Might there have been a downside to being in Charla's position—so well known, so closely watched?

The iconic image of the perky cheerleader who's elected homecoming queen carries a certain resonance for most American males, but I wouldn't have guessed the same was true for females. I learned the hard way that I was wrong. Once Charla agreed to dine with me, I shared the news of our pending "date" with several female friends, and their reaction was overwhelmingly negative.

I was taken aback at the vehemence of their disapproval. After all, these were good, supportive friends, none of whom had ever even met Charla. But she seemed to stir up memories of the cheerleaders and homecoming queens of their own youth, and they would cut her no slack. Told that I planned to explore the ups and downs of Charla's high school years, one replied, "Oh, you want us to feel sorry for Little Miss Homecoming Queen?" Another predicted, with some glee, that Charla would now be overweight. Meeow!

Charla is not the least bit surprised when she learns of my gal pals' reactions; she's had plenty of experience with such sentiments, it seems. "High school girls are the worst," she says, laughing. "They can be such bitches! They're just terrible. I had more friends that were boys. I just got along with them better, a lot of the time, than the girls. I think it's human nature, to a certain extent, if you were not up for homecoming queen or cheerleader or whatever, to resent those who were. Maybe you don't understand why it wasn't you in the spotlight, so you find fault with those who were. We've all reacted that way. I certainly have."

I remember how thrilled I was, at one point in my life, that Charla Hahn even knew who I was, that she might actually acknowledge me when we passed in the hall at school. That now strikes me as an odd sort of confirmational power to award to someone, and I suppose I shouldn't be surprised that there was a downside to holding that sort of influence. After all, I've seen my share of John Hughes films.

"There were horrible, horrible rumors," Charla recalls. "There was a time in high school when the rumor was that I'd had an abortion. I mean, I was a virgin all through high school, and here were people saying that I had been pregnant and had had an abortion. Some people seemed determined to hate you, even when you tried to be nice. So you'd have your little circle of friends that you tried to stay connected with, and then you'd do your best to be nice to everyone else."

I wonder if Charla ever felt trapped by her prominence at school. "Oh, absolutely. There were times when I told my mom, 'I wish I could just go to school and not have to worry about what I'm wearing and how my hair looks or that today's a ball game so I'm supposed to be up and feel good, no matter what.'

"But there were days when I didn't feel that pressure. I remember taking an anthropology class where there wasn't a soul that I knew. And I learned so much from those people that I had never run around with. That was an eye-opening experience. They were probably thinking, Oh, here's Miss Cheerleader. But I had a chance to just be myself, and I was grateful to them for letting me see the other side of things. They didn't care who I was. This was a class, that was what was important. So get down on your knees and start digging, you know? And it was wonderful. I loved it because nobody cared. For that hour every day, I could just be me, which brought a certain sense of freedom."

A teacher for nearly twenty years now—first seventh- and eighth-grade chemistry and biology, and now second- and third-grade physical education—Charla certainly understands the pressures young women continue to face: "My daughter's a cheerleader, and she also sings beautifully. And since she takes after her father, she's much taller than I am—she's about five-eight, compared to my five-two—and has played basketball and last year even threw the shot put. But this year, she's not going out for track and field because 'people in shot put are big,' she says. People have called her big. She's not fat but she's big. I think she's beautiful and I tell her so. 'Honey, you're beautiful. Don't listen to those people.' "

It occurs to me that Charla is now confronted with a challenge diametrically different from the one her own parents faced. Where they may have worried that Charla would come to value her attractiveness above her other good qualities, Charla is faced with convincing her own daughter that she's more attractive than she may currently be able to imagine herself. My own parents, I'm sure, can commiserate.

Things close early in Weatherford, Oklahoma, and it soon becomes clear that we're holding up the serving staff at the City Diner. So we call it a night, and I drive Charla home. I am introduced to two of her three kids (including her tall, talented daughter, who is indeed quite lovely and will, I hope, one day come to treasure every single one of her sixty-eight inches of height) before saying good night and heading home.

Like most of my first dates back in high school, this one ends without a good night kiss, but for once I'm acting out of propriety, not insecurity.

Four-Eyed and Forty

SOMEONE somewhere, worried that I might actually survive my fortieth birthday with my sunny disposition and positive attitude intact, saw to it that my eyesight underwent a rapid decline in the weeks leading up to the big day. So my birthday present to myself was a trip to the optometrist and my first pair of glasses.

It's odd how any slight alteration in our daily existence brings with it a sense of both excitement and anxiety. Whether you grow a beard, dye your hair blond, or strap on a pair of Rollerblades, you take on, by the very act, a new constituency. So suddenly, by slipping on these specs, I was not the man I'd been five minutes before; I was now someone who wore glasses, the newest member of a vast club.

As I wandered the streets of Manhattan, I found myself suddenly aware of everyone I passed and whether or not they were wearing glasses. Two hours previous, I wouldn't have taken note of such a seemingly insignificant detail. I almost expected some passing myopic to reveal some special mode of communication existing among my optically challenged brothers and sisters—a secret sign, some acknowledgment that yes, we were different but we were as one. However, if there exists such a sign, I've yet to suss it out. It seems that membership in this four-eyed fraternity offers few, if any, benefits. Not even a secret handshake. Of course, I couldn't help feeling a little twinge of resentment toward those two-eyed individuals I passed on the street. Never before did I realize just how blind those who see clearly without the aid of an ocular apparatus can be. They are clueless, as once was I, as to how good they have it.

I had actually been briefly excited about the prospect of needing glasses but only for the attention they'd bring. I've long coveted the fuss that temporary health care aids and accessories foster. There was a time in my youth when I longed for nothing so dearly as a cast. What could be better? After the initial pain of fracturing one's limb, one could settle back and bask in the attention that these plaster sheaths invariably elicit. And everyone likes to sign a cast, don't they? So even someone with a relatively small circle of friends can suddenly appear to be a Big Man—or Woman—on Campus.

I wonder, though, if deeply imbedded societal attitudes about glasses might now affect the way others perceive me. Will I, never an imposing physical specimen, now be pegged an especially easy mark by street toughs? Will I appear somehow bookish? Will strangers think me perhaps smarter than I am when first we meet? And most important, do women make passes at guys who wear glasses? It's too soon to tell on this last question, but early returns are not promising. Still, I'm keeping my fingers crossed. Perhaps that will prove to be the secret membership benefit I've been seeking.

Saturnal Cults

CALL me cold and uncaring if you will, but that certain Saturn ad not only fails to make me feel warm and cozy, it creeps me out. I'm referring to the one where the young woman is trying to get the hell out of a Saturn dealership with her new car.

I worry about that young woman; I hope she made it out with her sanity—nay, her very soul—intact. For in this ad, Saturn comes off as every bit as much a cult as a car company.

As the commercial opens, she's been waiting in isolation for, what, an hour? A day? A week? There's no way of knowing, but she certainly seems relieved at the opportunity for even minimal human contact. Have they even let her use the bathroom? I suspect not. A man enters, an artificial smile plastered on his face, a certain glassiness in his eye. "Are you ready to see your new car?" he asks, and though she tries to keep calm as she answers in the affirmative, I believe the subtext here is,

"Hell, yes, I'm ready to see my new car. I've been locked up in here for hours. Not a bite to eat, nothing to drink, not a frigging *Car and Driver*. What the hell are you people running here?"

But let's face it, even the strongest among us would wilt under the weight of such deprivation. It's a common syndrome among kidnap victims and others held captive against their will that they come to identify with their captors. So, though some voice of reason may still be crying out from deep within the soul of this poor victim, her defenses are down; she'll resort to anything to gain favor with her torturers, for how else might her torture cease?

"Are you excited?" the sinister one asks.

"I'm real excited," she says hopefully, doing her best to appease him. For if she is not enthusiastic, perhaps he will—oh, heaven let it not be so!—place her back in confinement until she bloody well *is* excited.

As they enter the room where her car awaits, there is a group gathered. Who are these people, and why are they here? Is this the first car this dealership has ever sold? Don't they have jobs to do? They surround the poor woman, the same sinister smiles on their faces that we saw on the first man's visage, and now that man, apparently the cult's leader, dangles the keys before the young woman—teasing, taunting, tormenting her a bit further. And before she can have those keys, he must first announce, "This is Ellen. And this is her first . . . new . . . car." The group applauds, perhaps only to muffle the rhythmic under-their-breath chanting—"One of us . . . one of us"—and

I fear, though I pray it's not true, that they are right, that she is now one of them.

I fully expect to one day see Ellen behind the wheel of that same Saturn, an eerie smile plastered on her own face, her glassy stare turned skyward as she watches, waiting, for a certain passing comet.

All I Want for Christmas Is My Two-Door Coupe

THE Christmas season is perhaps the clearest example of the malleability of time. As a child, I found that the days between Thanksgiving and Christmas stretched on and on, seemingly into infinity. Like Bill Murray's character in the film *Groundhog Day*, I arose each morn, only to find that no time had passed. Christmas was still eons away. My grandmother provided some reassurance with an annual gift of an Advent calendar. These featured little windows that were to be opened, one a day, each providing a sign to an anxious lad that the days were indeed passing, that I hadn't unknowingly entered some alternate dimension where time stands still. One glance at that calendar proved that, yes, at least a few of those two and a half dozen sunsets that stood between me and the Day of Days had indeed come and gone. I might just get there after all.

What I didn't know then—and learned too late—is the lesson that the late Harry Chapin articulated: It's got to be the going—not the getting there—that's good. I say I learned this too late because now that I'm an all-dues-paid, card-carrying member of the secret society of grown-ups, time plays an entirely different set of tricks on me. Nowadays, I go to bed on Thanksgiving night, full of turkey, pumpkin pie, and white Grenache, only to wake up the next day to discover that it's Christmas Eve and I've purchased not one of the several dozen gifts that are expected from me. Not a card has been mailed, no lights strung, no decorations hung. And I'm expected at three holiday parties in the next two hours.

I've been trying to pin down the precise moment in the course of a lifetime when this compression of time takes place. There's much study and research yet to be done in this arena, but early evidence clearly suggests a link between the length of an individual's gift wish list and the duration of the Yuletide. As a lad, the only problem I faced when compiling my list was gathering enough paper to accommodate my catalogue of demands. Nowadays, when asked what I'd like for Christmas, I affect a selflessness of Mother Teresan proportion, decrying the notion that I might have given any thought to my own needs and desires in this sacred season. "Oh, I don't know," goes my usual protest. "I don't really need anything, I'm sure I'll love whatever you choose." Of course, the truth is that this stance is less a matter of selflessness than surrender. None of my friends and loved ones can afford to present me with a Mercedes convertible, a month in Tahiti, or a loft in Tribeca, so why make them feel inadequate?

Promises Broken

ONE more New Year's Eve has come and gone, and as one walks the mean streets of the city, one encounters the discarded remnants of good intentions. The carcasses of resolutions that flowered with such promise just days ago now lie forgotten, lifeless; the butt of a cigarette settles into a crack in the sidewalk, discarded by a two-pack-a-day puffer who went cold turkey at 12:01 A.M. on January 1 but was lighting up again on the third. A grocery bag filled with empty beer cans is perched at the front door of the very man who was going to switch to nonalcoholic beer this year. A Big Mac carton whisks by, driven by the north wind. It was dropped inadvertently by the woman who promised herself she'd cut down on her fat intake this year and eat more vegetables. She'd intended to order a salad, but she had a coupon for the Big Mac and just one couldn't hurt, could it?

Lest you take my tone for one of superiority, I should admit here and now that my own powers of resolve have often been tested and found lacking in early January. I now take a different tack: starting small and aiming gradually higher with each passing year.

For instance, to start the new millennium right, I have resolved to make it all the way to January 1, 2001, without stealing a car. I'm pretty sure I'll make it, too.

You may scoff, but at the end of 2000, I'll be able to look back and say, "Yes! I did it!" I'll end the old year and begin the new one with a sense of accomplishment and pride, while others are attempting to assuage their feelings of guilt and failure in therapies of various ilk. Then, in the year 2001, I can tackle that hard-to-kick shoplifting habit and start paying for my Céline Dion CDs.

Is it any wonder we find those New Year's resolutions hard to keep? They are born of disappointment. New Year's Eve has proven, through the years, to have more potential for utter disappointment than any other holiday one can name. The buildup is always promising; in cinema, story, and song, we're fed images of lavish parties held in beautifully appointed homes; of ritzy clubs packed with gorgeous, stylishly dressed couples living . . . laughing . . . *loving*; of delectable, delicious alcoholic concoctions that lend warm feelings of goodwill and well-being; of good times being had by all!

But oh, the heartache of promises broken; most often one finds the only invitation received is to a soirée thrown by a friend of a friend's brother. Upon arriving, you find you know no one else in the tiny space—"We call it the family room, but it's really just a converted garage. Did the work myself, y'know!"—save the friend or loved one you brought along. Instead of attractive and tasty hors d'oeuvres and a chilled flute filled with vintage champagne, you're handed a can of lukewarm Meisterbrau and steered toward a table holding three bowls of Doritos—Cool Ranch, Nacho Cheese, and Original flavors, each staler than the last.

The other guests appear to have been drinking since last New Year's Eve and so are finding it difficult to make intelligent—or even intelligible—conversation. So you and your companion hole up in a corner, vowing to yourselves that you won't go through this again next year. Next year you'll throw your own party, invite all your favorite people, maybe even have the affair catered with a professional bartender and tray after tray of scrumptious appetizers carried about by uniformed attendants. Why, it'll be the party of the year!

And you—you'll look great! After all, by then you'll have given up smoking, cut way back on your drinking, and lost twenty pounds, thanks to your new low-fat diet and regimen of daily exercise! And me, I'll have shoplifted my last Céline Dion CD.

Hollywood, Heal Thyself

MUCH wringing of the hands occurs these days concerning the effect the profligate depiction of graphic violence in modern films may be having on our youth. This may strike some as a legitimate concern, but I view the outcry over onscreen violence as an orchestrated effort to provide a smoke screen, concealing a trend that poses a far greater threat to our collective well-being and sense of public decency. I refer, of course, to the recent disturbing proliferation of graphic vomit scenes in movies. I feel the time has come for the movie industry to police itself and, if it will not, for the federal government to intervene on behalf of the American moviegoing public—yes, even the worldwide community of film lovers.

Persuasive arguments can be constructed for both sides of this volatile issue: There's a faction that claims that cinematic regurgitation encourages vomiting on our streets, and an opposing camp, which opines that the viewing of vomiting in movie theatres provides a release for such impulses, thereby leading to a decline in potential real-life purging.

Surely no one can dispute, however, the visceral reaction we all experience when we witness the tossing of cookies on the big screen. Who among us doesn't get a bit queasy at such moments? Who doesn't feel at least the fleeting impulse toward the sort of copycat behavior against which naysayers of cinematic violence warn? I assure you it will only take one impressionable moviegoer, unable to control that all-too-natural gag reflex, to create a veritable flood of lost lunches. Can any of us pretend to be of such strong stock that we could witness a fellow multiplex patron invoking the name of Ralph into a giant tub of popcorn and not follow suit?

Lest anyone decry my stance as pro-censorship, let me say that I support free expression for artists of every stripe. Still, with freedom comes responsibility, and it's time the world's filmmakers were held responsible for their excesses. I'm not suggesting that the film industry institute a specific code—reminiscent of the production code enforced by the Hays Office in the 1930s and '40s—that would cleanse tomorrow's films of all regurgitation. Instead, I propose, as a solution to this burgeoning crisis, an addition to the already existing canon of movie ratings. Let us add a new subcategory: GR for "graphic regurgitation." This would be used in conjunction with the established ratings of G, PG, PG-13, R, NC-17, and X. Suppose, say, a new Leonardo DiCaprio film came out that contained no violence, no profanity, no nudity or adult situations, but did contain a depiction of Hollywood's boy-king blowing chunks. This film would be assigned a G, with a subrating of GR. This would allow concerned parents to make informed decisions as to whether this film is suitable for their children and if, perhaps, a side trip to the drugstore to pick up some Pepto-Bismol isn't called for.

On the other end of the spectrum, imagine that the script for *Die Hard 7* called for Bruce Willis's struggle against Latvian terrorists to be temporarily derailed by the ingestion of a bad clam. The producers of that film could then count on an R-GR rating, the R for the inevitable senseless slaughter of the aforementioned Latvians and dozens of innocent bystanders, the GR for the tainted-clam purging scene.

Again, far be it from me to demand that those who favor realistic on-screen depictions of digestive distress be deprived of the opportunity. I'm only suggesting that those of more genteel sensibilities be offered due warning. The time has come, Hollywood. Heal thyself. Or, at the very least, hurl off-camera.

In tribute to my mother, a breast cancer survivor, a percentage of my profits from sales of this book will go to benefit breast cancer research. In turn, I ask you to please consider donating your money or time to a local breast cancer research organization in your area.

About the Author

BRETT LEVERIDGE is the man behind the award-winning website BRETTnews (www.brettnews.com). He has also written for many other print and online publications, and is an occasional contributor to the nationally syndicated radio program This American Life *and National Public Radio's* All Things Considered. *Born and raised in Oklahoma City, Leveridge now lives in New York City. He can be reached via e-mail at: brett@brettnews.com.*